Holding Up the Sky

YOUNG PEOPLE
IN CHINA

Margaret Rau

LODESTAR BOOKS   E. P. Dutton   New York

LIBRARY OF CONGRESS CATALOGING IN PUBLICATION DATA
Rau, Margaret.
Holding up the sky.
"Lodestar Books."
Summary: Describes the lives of several young people
in various parts of China, and the political, cultural,
and economic factors that affect them.
1. Youth—China—Case studies—Juvenile literature.
2. China—Social conditions—Case studies—Juvenile
literature. [1. Youth—China. 2. China—Social
conditions] I. Title.
HQ799.C55R38 1983 305.2'35'0951 82-20959
ISBN 0-525-66718-0

Published in the United States by E. P. Dutton, Inc.,
2 Park Avenue, New York, N.Y. 10016

Editor: Virginia Buckley   Designer: Trish Parcell
Printed in the U.S.A.   First Edition

10 9 8 7 6 5 4 3 2

for Cathy Wulff

I would like to acknowledge the skill and creative genius in the darkroom work of Diane Lewis, who has brought out all the latent qualities of the images captured by my camera during my journeys around China.

Contents

FOREWORD

This is a book about young people of China. Some live in the cities, others in the countryside. Not all of them can be represented, for China, which contains one-fourth of the world's population, is the third largest country in the world, with wide expanses and many kinds of regions. The young people who live in the coastal areas have a different outlook from those who live in the hinterlands. Young peasants differ widely in their life-styles from their counterparts in the cities. But life in the countryside can also vary. Some farming areas are rich, others poor. Some profit by being close to large cities such as Shanghai and Beijing (Peking). Others are located in places that are far removed from coastal influences.

China's poorest area, the northwest loess region, has been subjected to periodic famines for centuries. Those who till the soil here must constantly battle soil erosion, droughts, and flash floods.

Most Chinese are members of the Han nationality, so Hans are known as the majority people. But China also has many smaller groups that are not Han. They are known as the minority peoples. There are some fifty-seven different minority peoples. They have their own customs and, in most cases, their own language. This book can cover only a few of these nationalities.

But whether the young people of China belong to one of the minorities or to the majority, whether they live in the coastal cities or the distant hinterlands, it is their vitality and energy that will guide China in days to come. It is on their shoulders that the responsibility will fall for holding up the sky of their country.

PRONUNCIATION GUIDE

In this book, I have used China's new form of phonetic spelling. The old spelling is being retained in regard to historical happenings and places. But modern-day names have been spelled the new way. The following guide should help the reader in determining the correct pronunciation.

a   Vowel as in *far*

b   Consonant as in *be*

c   Consonant as in *its*

ch   Consonant as in *church,* strongly aspirated

d   Consonant as in *do*

e   Vowel as in *her*

f   Consonant as in *foot*

g   Consonant as in *go*

h   Consonant as in *her,* strongly aspirated

i   Vowel as in *eat* or as in *sir* (when in syllables beginning with c, ch, r, s, sh, z and zh)

j   Consonant as in *jeep*

k   Consonant as in *kind,* strongly aspirated

l   Consonant as in *land*

m   Consonant as in *me*

n   Consonant as in *no*

o   Vowel as in *law*

p   Consonant as in *par,* strongly aspirated

q   Consonant as in *cheek*

r   Consonant as in *right* (not rolled) or pronounced as z in *azure*

s   Consonant as in *sister*

sh   Consonant as in *shore*

t   Consonant as in *top,* strongly aspirated

u   Vowel as in *too,* also as in the French *tu* or the German *München*

v   Consonant used only to produce foreign words, national minority words and local dialects

w   Semi-vowel in syllables beginning with u when not preceded by consonants, as in *want*

x   Consonant as in *she*

y   Semi-vowel in syllables beginning with i or u when not preceded by consonants, as in *yet*

z   Consonant as in *zero*

zh   Consonant as in *jump*

Source: Adapted from *Beijing Review*

Factory Worker Chung Huaping

Twenty-two-year-old Chung Huaping pedals his bicycle furiously as he races the clock to get to work on time. Like all Chinese, young Chung puts his last name first. His given name is Huaping. Huaping has gotten an early start, for he has a long distance to cover to reach the suburban factory where he is employed.

During his six-day work week, Huaping will live in a rented room in one of the dormitory buildings that the factory runs for its employees. Living at the dormitory is optional, and some people prefer housing in nearby apartments. But rent is cheaper in the dormitories, which are on the factory grounds and just a step away from work. However, Huaping likes to get a break from his daily routines by spending Sunday, his day off, with his family at their home in the inner city of Shanghai.

Shanghai, with some eleven million people, is the biggest city in China and one of the largest in the world. It stands on the Huangpu

River, a small tributary near the mouth of the Yangtze, China's most important waterway. The city owes its Western skyline of massive Victorian-style buildings and modest early American skyscrapers to the days when foreigners lived and did business there. When the People's Republic of China was founded in 1949, the foreigners were asked to go, and the buildings are now occupied by Chinese officials.

But the foreigners left a legacy greater than their buildings. They introduced factories to the city. Today Shanghai has become the country's foremost manufacturing center. It is the second largest steel-producing city in China. Many different kinds of petrochemicals, as well as cars and trucks, radios and television sets, steam turbines, electric motors, heavy machinery, and machine tools are also made there.

Huaping's destination is the Shanghai Machine Tools Factory. He feels lucky to have this job, for recently Shanghai has had a high unemployment rate. But his good fortune isn't exactly due to luck. His father, who had several years yet before retirement at sixty, decided to quit early and pass his job at the factory along to Huaping.

Shanghai wakes up early. By dawn almost everyone is out exercising. Exercising became the fashion in 1952 when Chairman Mao Zedong proclaimed: Promote Physical Culture and Build Up the People's Health. Following his dictate, exercises of all kinds were introduced in schools, factories, fields, and offices. But people also began to get up early to do some jogging or calisthenics on their own before going to work or school. The elderly prefer taijiquan (tai chi chuan), a set of movements from ancient China. Young people like brisk modern exercises.

By seven o'clock most of the exercisers have disappeared, and the streets have become jammed with people heading for work. Packed buses rattle along, blaring their horns. Whistles of river ferries mingle with the melancholy blasts of steamships. But most of the vehicles are bicycles. Like a tide they flow through the streets, bells ringing in a jingling jangling chorus of sound.

It takes skill to cycle in this swarm, and the riders have to weave

Young men in a city high school do brisk calisthenics before their classes begin. All over China, high school students start the day with exercise as part of the national campaign to promote physical health.

from side to side to avoid hitting one another or pedestrians attempting to cross the street. Police officers direct traffic at the most congested corners.

Huaping steers his bicycle deftly among the others. His way leads him along the shore road, or bund, as it is called. It skirts the tawny waters of the Huangpu and is bordered by the stately buildings of another era. Already there's a haze of blue smog in the air. It will increase as the hot muggy day progresses. Shanghai has been plagued with a high concentration of air pollution for years. And many of its citizens suffer from respiratory illnesses. Other cities that are becoming industrialized are also having a growing smog problem.

In September of 1979, the government adopted its first environmental protection law, which lays out certain rules for factories to follow. In 1980, the nation launched a publicity campaign to explain the need for such protection, with television and radio speakers all over the country describing the harm pollution does to people's health. Huaping's own factory has experts studying its problem.

Huaping reaches the bridge that spans the Huangpu just below the mouth of one of its small tributaries, Suzhou Creek. Junks, brown sails spread, and tugboats, hauling long lines of loaded barges, are traveling downstream on their way to the docks. Here they will discharge their stores—everything from lumber and fresh vegetables to bags of grain, bales of cotton, and silk skeins—for use in city markets and textile plants.

Beyond the bridge the traffic becomes even denser. Suddenly Huaping is passed by a young man who is speeding along on a motorbike with such ease that Huaping feels a quick stab of envy. Then he grins to himself. Now that he has a job, he can save his money and buy a motorbike for himself one day. After all, it was his savings that purchased the bike he is riding now. Of course the motorbike will be much more expensive, so it will take him longer to save the money, but by being frugal he can do it eventually.

Along the Shanghai waterfront, barges bring in rice, bales of silk and cotton, and vegetables from the north.

Wrapped in his dream of the motorbike, Huaping forgets to keep an eye out for pedestrians. He narrowly misses an old woman who, market basket over her arm, is flapping around him like a wounded duck, cackling out in fear and anger. Huaping stops as a policeman approaches. Gravely the policeman inspects Huaping's license, issued to him when he registered his bicycle. The license is in order, so the policeman checks his brakes and his bell. Then he asks Huaping severely if he's been drinking and reminds him that cyclists who've had too much aren't allowed on bicycles. Finally the policeman gives him a severe lecture on endangering human life and limb. He warns Huaping that more violations such as this one may cause his license to be taken away for a month.

By this time a crowd has gathered. And the old woman, in her shrill voice, tells each newcomer who comes up the whole story of how this thoughtless young man almost ran her down. The policeman has to wave everyone on before Huaping has a clear path ahead.

Delayed by the crowd and the policeman's lecture, Huaping barely makes it to work on time. He parks and locks his bicycle in the factory parking lot. Then he dashes through the factory's wide entranceway. Here a large red poster reads: Put out every effort to bring about the Four Modernizations: Modernization of Agriculture! Modernization of Industry! Modernization of Science! Modernization of Defense!

Huaping has heard a great deal about the Four Modernizations as China strives to bring herself to the level of the developed nations. All the workers in his plant are being urged to do their part by raising production. Workers who overfulfill the monthly quota set by the government are paid bonuses equaling 10 percent of their monthly wages. Those that overfulfill the quota each month for a year receive an additional bonus amounting to 5 percent of their yearly wages.

Huaping is a member of one of the many work teams in the factory. At first the others were skeptical of his ability to take his father's place, but they're quite satisfied now. He's a conscientious worker. And though in the beginning he was slow, with practice and

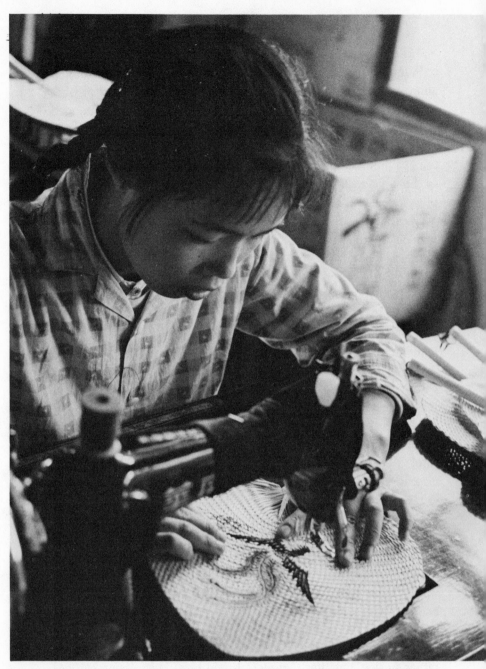

A young woman sews appliqués on a palm leaf fan that will probably be exported as one of China's handicrafts.

experience he has been able to earn bonuses for two consecutive months. His regular salary is about 50 yuan (25 American dollars) a month. But the bonuses bring up his earnings.

Huaping also has been able to hold his own in the series of contests being held among the factory's various work teams. The red flag that hangs in the workshop of his team proclaims their victory in the last contest.

This month the factory has introduced another campaign. It's directed against accidents. Factory managers decided there were too many of these a year—more than a hundred. Some were minor ones, such as abrasions of feet and hands. Others were far more serious. Most accidents were due to the workers' carelessness.

For instance, though protective goggles are provided for those who must handle welding torches, some of the young people see no need to use them until, too late, a flying spark seriously damages their eyes. Others who are working at heights sometimes forget to put on safety collars and belts. And many are careless near moving machinery, giving it a chance to catch and crush their feet, fingers, hands, or arms.

To impress the need for caution, the factory is currently holding classes on safety. Posters are set up in prominent places: No Accidents Within a Hundred Days. The workers are warned that if they endanger this record during the campaign, their bonuses will be reduced.

In his haste to keep up his speed, Huaping doesn't take time to put on his goggles while he's welding, and an overseer catches him. He's given a sharp scolding and told that his bonus will be reduced for the oversight. Huaping is chagrined—two rebukes in one day.

Huaping's factory is government-owned and run. Its workers include some highly placed Communist Party representatives who do the same work as the others. By their example, they are expected to provide the rest of the employees with the incentive to fulfill the quotas and goals set by the government. They also make periodic reports to the government, especially if the factory is being poorly operated.

An in-factory trade union serves the workers. It helps arbitrate any disputes over unfair practices that arise between the factory directors and foremen and the workers. But the union is primarily concerned with the welfare of its members. Every factory in China has such a union, and every worker belongs to it. The union is run by a chairman, several vice-chairmen, and an overall committee that assigns working committees to carry out the union's various duties.

Huaping pays a small sum in union dues. It amounts to 5 percent of his monthly wages. Out of its profits, the factory contributes a much larger share to the fund, and the government, as owner of the factory, also pays into it.

Part of the fund is used for education—special courses, lectures, and part-time schools for the workers. Some goes to maintaining a factory library and a workers' cultural center, with basketball courts, table tennis equipment, and a swimming pool. Films are shown and live entertainment is given in the amusement hall. There's a television set in the factory lounge. The union fund is also used to help members out of financial difficulties.

Factory management and the trade union cooperate in providing the facilities and staff for a day-care nursery-kindergarten, which takes in the workers' preschool children. Huaping's young married friends keep their children there. This enables both parents to work. Women have fifty-six days' maternity leave at full wages after the birth of their babies. When they return to work, they can leave their babies at the nursery. Twice a day they are given half-hour free periods to breast-feed their children.

In the nursery room, rows of round-faced babies lie placidly in cribs. In the kindergarten, small children wearing starched pinafores play games. In another room, children who are turning six recite from a blackboard and flash cards. They count, add simple figures, and read a few Chinese characters. They're taught simple hygiene rules—to wash their hands before eating and to brush their teeth daily. The trained practical nurses in charge hold clinics to discuss child care with the mothers.

Huaping's father tells him he should be proud of his factory, which provides many fine services. Not all places of work, especially those in smaller towns, are able to do so much for their employees. Some factories charge a small yearly insurance fee of 5 yuan (2½ American dollars) for the medical services they provide. But the workers in the Shanghai Machine Tools Factory have free medical care, including operations and lengthy hospitalizations, during which they continue to receive their salaries.

If they should need long recuperation periods, they may be sent to the factory-run sanitarium for workers. When they retire at sixty years of age, they receive pensions that range from 60 to 100 percent of their wages, depending on the length of their service.

Huaping eats in the factory-run canteen, where workers get inexpensive meals. The cooks in the huge kitchen are jolly and efficient, bustling to and fro in their white aprons and caps, wielding gigantic ladles, strainers, forks, knives, and choppers. As noon approaches, great pots of rice and noodles and dumplings bubble on the stoves. Meat and vegetable dishes are stewing in huge pans. Chefs remove the last trays of freshly baked loaves of bread from the ovens just as the factory whistle blows.

Huaping lines up with the other workers at the food counters. The queue is made up mostly of young people. The older ones have a separate lunchroom because many of them have stomach problems and require bland food that is specially prepared for them. The lunch period is only forty-five minutes long, so to save time, workers purchase food chips in advance. This enables the line to move more quickly, because it isn't necessary to make change. Huaping orders a simple meal of noodles and vegetables—no meat today. He is thinking of the reduced bonus he will get because of his carelessness. Somehow the meal doesn't seem as tasty as usual.

Huaping's day ends at 4:30 P.M. Sometimes he stays later to attend political sessions held by the Communist Party representatives. Often union officials hold discussions on the Four Modernizations. Sometimes the sessions last almost until suppertime.

Huaping's dormitory has a communal kitchen as well as communal showers and toilets. But Huaping prefers not to cook for himself. Instead he buys something from the canteen, which is open twenty-four hours a day. Huaping usually eats his meal in the tiny room he shares with another young man. Between them, the two pay about 2 yuan (1 American dollar) rent per month for the room and less than ½ a yuan for gas, electricity, and water.

A separate dormitory houses the women. Other buildings, with two- and even three-bedroom apartments, are for married couples and their families. The rent is higher there, but it's still quite reasonable.

After dinner, Huaping may read or, if he's very tired, go to bed. Often he spends his evenings in the factory lounge, where he watches television. Sometimes he and his friends get up a fast game of basketball. If the weather is warm, they go swimming in the pool.

Whenever the factory engineers hold courses to teach specialized skills, Huaping takes them, because he knows it will give him a chance to improve his position in the factory. One day he will marry, and he wants to be well along in his career by that time. Young people are told to work hard and improve themselves to help their country achieve the Four Modernizations, but Huaping knows that doing so will be to his advantage also.

The Great Proletarian Cultural Revolution

Twenty-four-year-old Wang Meiling and twenty-three-year-old Yu Shaoli are doing a brisk business at their little portable food stand in the park near their home. Whenever the days are hot and muggy, the wilted city folk are attracted to one of the many Shanghai parks.

The parks are especially crowded during the two-hour siesta period between noon and two. Then elderly people in sober blue jackets and trousers stroll along with their small grandchildren. Brightly dressed grade-school children accompanied by their teacher flutter over the paths like butterflies. Clusters of laughing young people—girls in one group, boys in another—stroll by. More rarely, a boy and girl walk along together hand in hand.

Most of the girls have their hair bobbed or in short braids. They are dressed in pants or cotton skirts and pretty flowered shirts. A few teenagers are wearing jeans. Almost everyone wears cloth slippers, tennis shoes, or heelless plastic sandals.

Schoolgirls stroll in a park during siesta time, which lasts from noon until two.

Some of the office women, however, are more fashionably dressed and have neatly waved permanented hair. Permanent waves have become quite popular in China. The women may also be wearing a little makeup—powder, pale rouge, and light lipstick—and some clatter along in heels. Most men are in short sleeves and slacks, but a few have on business suits and ties. Shanghai has the most cosmopolitan look of any city in China.

Meiling and Shaoli's little stand is a popular attraction. With their hair in short pigtails tied with bright ribbons, the young women look younger than their age. They serve everything from sweet rice cakes and salted sunflower or pumpkin seeds to ice-cream bars on a stick, with an occasional cup of tea which they pour from a thermos bottle.

By late afternoon they have sold out their stock, so they trundle their portable snack bar from the park and down the street toward home. They live in a neighborhood of old houses whose walls line the quiet lanes of one of Shanghai's residential districts. They pass a child pedaling up and down the cobblestone lane on a new tricycle. Several older boys playing toss ball stop to stare at the young vendors, mouths watering for an ice-cream bar.

Already the bustle of suppertime is filling the lanes. Chattering women gathered around the public faucet are drawing water for the evening meal. Though newer apartments have running water and flush toilets, many of the older houses are not equipped with plumbing. The toilets in these homes are only wooden seats placed over old-fashioned slop jars. Later tonight the contents of the slop jars will be poured into larger containers and set in front of the doors for the predawn night soil (human waste) collectors, who will empty the contents of the jars into their huge metal containers. When they have finished their rounds, they will cart their odorous loads off to the country to be used as fertilizer.

Meiling and Shaoli stop at the neighborhood community hall to chat a minute with Mrs. Lao, who is head of the committee that runs the neighborhood. Each city neighborhood has a committee made up of residents who have been elected by the people among whom they live. They are usually retirees and, like Mrs. Lao, are highly respected for their integrity and understanding. Their headquarters is the community hall, which is equipped with books, periodicals, and a television set.

Young and elderly of the neighborhood refer to Mrs. Lao as Old Auntie Lao. The word *Old* is a title like the western *Honorable.* It doesn't apply to age particularly, but to those who are respected for their wisdom. Thus a professor of thirty-five will be called Old Master. While "Old" is a term of respect in China, "Auntie" is a term of affection. It is applied to older women who have earned their place in the hearts of their community.

Old Auntie Lao is especially concerned about the young people of her neighborhood. The ordeal of the Great Proletarian Cultural Revolution between 1966 and 1976 has left deep scars in the minds

Hovels such as these are preserved to remind people of the horrible living conditions in Shanghai before the establishment of the People's Republic in 1949.

of those who lived through that era. Like many others in China, Mrs. Lao is haunted by the ten dreadful years.

The Cultural Revolution was launched by Mao Zedong, then Chairman of the Communist Party and accepted leader of the country. At that time, production was increasing on farms and in city factories. Universities were beginning to vie in quality with their Western counterparts. But Mao Zedong felt a revolution was necessary because it seemed to him that the country was slipping away from true communism. He ordered schools closed. Students were formed into an organization called the Red Guards. Indoctrination classes were held, using as text a little red book of Mao's sayings compiled by Lin Biao, then head of the People's Liberation Army, the military branch of the government.

Finally the students were sent out to spread the revolution. They were able to commandeer trains for free passage from place to place around the country. Some of the children who joined the crusade were only eight years old. Singing revolutionary hymns and chanting slogans from their little red books, the students began breaking into homes, museums, and ancient temples, smashing every foreign object and Chinese antique they could find. They were encouraged by Lin Biao and Jiang Qing (Chiang Ching), wife of Mao Zedong. She was aided by three powerful accomplices—Yao Wenyuan, Wang Hongwen, and Zhang Chunqiao (Chunchiao). They came to be called the Gang of Four.

With no one to check them, the students began persecuting respected Party officials, professors, businessmen, workers—anyone who crossed them in any way. Their excuse was always that these people were bad Communists.

Wang Meiling was taken out of school and punished by the authorities because she wrote a letter to an aunt who lives in America. Meiling's letter was opened in the post office. Even though it was just a friendly little note, the censor decided it was treasonable to be writing at all to someone in the United States. Meiling was made to pay for it by being sent to the countryside to work on a farm for the rest of her life. Shaoli was sent away too, because she was Meiling's friend.

Meiling remembers how frightened she was of the strange surroundings and of the peasants who were continually complaining because she didn't know how to do things properly. They made it plain they didn't want her there. No matter how hard she tried, she could not please anyone. She still recalls the humiliating criticisms she had to keep making of herself in an effort to appease them.

The Red Guards were only pawns in a power play between two factions in the Communist Party. One was led by Mao Zedong, the other by Liu Shaoji. Liu Shaoji was Chairman of the Standing Committee of the National People's Congress, which, with the Communist Party, governed the country. As Chairman of the National People's Congress, as well as of the Standing Committee, Liu Shaoji had power almost equal to that of Mao Zedong. In time, with the backing of Jiang Qing, the students were able to arrest Liu Shaoji, humiliate him publicly, and then privately torture him to death.

But such violence created more violence. The Red Guards split into factions which began fighting among themselves. They also began fighting with workers and peasants. Auntie Lao remembers the shouting, the gunfire, and the screams that went on day and night in the streets of Shanghai. Hospitals and morgues filled. People cowered in their homes, afraid to go out.

The same kind of fighting flared up all over China. At last the turmoil became so violent that Chairman Mao and other Party leaders, including Jiang Qing, became alarmed and ordered the People's Liberation Army, which had helped launch the Red Guard movement, to put an end to it. The Red Guards were disbanded. During the winter of 1968–69, some twenty million of them were sent to distant rural areas and told they must spend their lives working among the peasants. Their education was over.

Schools were reopened for the rest of the children, but the students still held power over the teachers, who were too afraid to impose discipline. The number of years spent at school was reduced from twelve to nine. And the curriculum was geared to practical rather than scientific research, with workers and peasants often serving as teachers.

Students were required to put in a great number of hours a week doing factory or farm work. They also had to give two to three months of every year to helping out in the fields or a factory. After they graduated from high school, they had to spend at least two years doing manual labor. Then they could apply to a university. But admission was uncertain, no longer dependent on entrance examinations. Instead, pupils had to be recommended by the people among whom they worked. Children from peasant or worker backgrounds or young soldiers from the People's Liberation Army were supposed to have first chance. But actually those chosen were members of families who were loyal to Jiang Qing and her accomplices.

Many professors were demoted and sent to the countryside to work. University training, including medical school, was reduced to two or, at the most, three years. All private businesses and services were shut down. This was called Cutting Off Capitalist Tails. Workers in factories were paid whether they worked or loafed. This was called To Each According to His Need, From Each According to His Ability. Many of the factories slowed to a halt, as workers spent their days discussing communism instead of doing their jobs. Exports fell drastically.

In the countryside, peasants were told what to plant, even if the soil and climate were not suitable for those crops. Production fell. Food became so scarce that people had to be issued ration cards to obtain even scanty amounts of what was available. They were told that this state of affairs was natural because communism meant living an austere life without comforts. Pretty clothes, permanent waves, cosmetics, and Western-style dress were all banned. Scarcely any consumer goods were available.

Revolutionary committees were set up in city and countryside. The committees were the forerunners of the present-day neighborhood committees. Old Auntie Lao had not been a member of the revolutionary committee in her neighborhood. Its members had been selected only on the approval of Jiang Qing's followers.

The revolutionary committees not only ran the affairs of the neighborhoods and spied into people's private lives but also held long political meetings which every adult in the neighborhood was required to attend. During the meetings, people were expected to criticize themselves for real or imaginary faults. They could also expect to be criticized by neighbors. Often people who held grudges used these occasions to get even.

Old Auntie Lao remembers the cloud of distrust that hung over everyone. People were afraid to talk to friends, even to members of their own family, especially their children, for fear that what they said would be repeated and used against them. A simple complaint or politically unwise remark, idly spoken, could cause one to lose a job or be jailed or exiled to the country.

By this time Jiang Qing, using the prestige of her husband's name, had taken almost complete control of the country. Mao Zedong, too old and ill to stop her, warned her that she and her three accomplices were headed for a downfall. The army commander, Lin Biao, was already dead. In 1971 he had been discovered plotting to kill Mao. He had tried to escape to the Soviet Union but had died in an airplane crash on the border of Outer Mongolia.

Then in 1976, Chairman Mao Zedong died, and before the Gang of Four could consolidate their power, they were taken into custody by Hua Guofeng, whom Mao Zedong had named as his successor. At the same time, followers of the clique were arrested all across the country. The revolutionary committees were replaced by neighborhood committees elected by the people themselves. Old Auntie Lao was made chairman of the new committee in her neighborhood and has remained so ever since.

Mrs. Lao is a Communist Party member. But not everyone on her committee belongs to the Party. Most of the members are older retired people. They donate their time to serving their community. They have many chores. Among other services, they run a day-care center for small children whose parents work at places that don't provide nurseries. They arbitrate neighborhood and family quarrels and are always ready to give help and advice when needed. They are also responsible for the community's health.

The committee members were presented with many problems caused by the Cultural Revolution when a freer era began. People started speaking out bitterly against the injustices they had suffered during the Cultural Revolution. Hordes of gaunt, ragged peasants marched on Beijing to complain about conditions in the countryside that had resulted in near famine. Thousands of young people like Meiling and Shaoli, along with members of the Red Guards, who had been banished from their homes in the cities, began to return. But there was no work for them. And their families didn't have room to put them up or food to give them from their own scanty supplies. Though the young people also had ration cards, they could be used only in the villages from which they had run away. Turned out of their former homes, disillusioned and starving, the young people began forming gangs that drifted through the large cities. With knives for weapons, they stole what they needed and slept where they could—under bridges, on park benches, in doorways.

Meiling finally ran away from the village where she had been living when a toothless old peasant whose wife had died tried to force her to marry him. Shaoli accompanied her. Both girls were welcomed by their families, but there was not enough food for them.

Auntie Lao came to their aid by looking into opportunities that were opening up under the new government. One of the first things the government had done was to lift the ban on privately run businesses. It was encouraging people to ease the massive unemployment situation by opening small grocery shops and food stands. Those who had special skills were urged to resume their services again. And city streets began flowering with watch-repairers, cobblers, photographers, even tooth-pullers—those ready dentists whose office equipment consists of a stool and a pair of pliers.

Young people especially were being encouraged to help solve the unemployment problem by creating jobs for themselves. Old Auntie Lao suggested that Meiling and Shaoli open a snack bar in the park. She even went with them to the district office to help them get the license that would allow them to stock up on goods from the government's wholesale warehouses. And she accompanied them to the park to select the best spot for their stand.

Above, *this man has one of the many small businesses that have sprung up since the end of the Cultural Revolution. He repairs shoes and makes leather goods.* Below, *these cooks have set up a little cooperative restaurant outside a temple museum. Visitors enjoy their deep-fried crullers, cakes, and tea.*

That had been several years ago. Meiling and Shaoli were so successful that they expanded their little business by bringing in other young people and forming a cooperative. Instead of one snack bar, the cooperative started to operate several around the neighborhood. After paying a low income tax to the government and putting aside some of the money to replenish their stock, the members divided the rest among themselves. The cooperative gave each person a steady though modest income.

The economy was picking up again. People had more money to spend, and factories were stepping up production of consumer goods. Stores were now stocked with such things as radios, bicycles, watches, textiles, even color television sets. And most goods had come off the ration lists.

As Auntie Lao reviews the changes of the past few years, a face suddenly rises before her mind's eye. It is the face of young Shen Tiyi, who had been only five when the Cultural Revolution began. Auntie Lao remembers him well—a bright-eyed inquisitive little boy with a cheery smile.

But as the Revolution got into full swing, Tiyi was sucked into the turmoil. When older children began persecuting their teachers, he joined in readily. As Tiyi grew older, he became one of the worst students in his school. His rowdy, arrogant ways gained him the admiration of many of his classmates. His teachers feared him.

When the Gang of Four was arrested in 1976, things changed. Teachers once more had control of their classes. They expected their students to study, and they enforced discipline. But Tiyi, who was now fifteen, continued to be insolent in class and to pick fights with younger children. He began playing truant from school and started thieving to get extra pocket money.

His teachers tried to help him. Old Auntie Lao counseled him too. She told him about her own childhood, how she had had to work in one of Shanghai's textile mills for mere pennies, sleeping on the cold floor, getting hardly anything to eat, beaten if she fell behind in her work.

"Many children died from such treatment," she told the boy,

"but I managed to stay alive. Then the Communist Party and Chairman Mao Zedong came along and liberated us all. And we worked together to change our whole city, our whole country. This is what you must do too, Tiyi."

Even while Old Auntie Lao was speaking, she had seen the cynical expression on Tiyi's face.

"Things have changed, Old Auntie," he told her. "The Party has changed. One day it calls us out to make revolution, and the next day it punishes us for it. It doesn't care about us."

By the time Tiyi was seventeen, his behavior had become so bad that he was sent to the work-study boarding school which the government had set up in 1978 for juvenile delinquents. Tiyi stayed there six months and then was released for good behavior. But he was continually sent back to the school.

Finally when Tiyi was nineteen, he held up and robbed a worker. He was given a three-year sentence at a juvenile reformatory for older offenders. Again he served his time and was released. Work was found for him. But shortly afterward, he quit his job and went back on the streets again. In the course of a robbery, he beat a young worker almost to death.

This time authorities gave up on him and sent him to a prison farm in the remote western hinterlands. There in the midst of a desert that is blazing hot in summer and freezing cold in winter, far away from home and comfort, Tiyi has to labor at reclaiming the wastelands. He has little chance of parole, no chance at all of escape. Auntie Lao knows about the hard life he is leading, because it has been well publicized in newspapers to warn other young delinquents of their fate if they don't reform.

So much going to waste, Auntie Lao thinks, remembering the Lost Generation, as some refer to them. Even in my darkest days, the Party could give me hope. But during the time of the Gang of Four, what could Tiyi and the others hope for?

"The Party failed him. I failed him," Auntie Lao whispers, tears running down her wrinkled cheeks. "Because I am a Party member, I am responsible too. I must share the blame."

The Neighborhood

Meiling slips through the doorway of her home to be greeted by fragrant odors drifting from the dark stuffy kitchen. Her father is bustling over the little gas stove where a pot of rice is bubbling. He is vigorously stirring some vegetables and shredded pork that he is frying in the big wok.

Meiling's father is one of the shipbuilders in the yards downstream. This day he had the early shift, so it is his turn to cook. Sometimes Meiling's mother, who works at a cooperative making children's clothes, comes home early and takes care of the kitchen chores. Sometimes it's Meiling's turn, sometimes her older brother Daming's. Holai, Meiling's twelve-year-old sister, helps by doing the shopping for the evening meal and putting the rice on to boil.

Holai is in junior middle school (junior high as it's called in the United States). She gets a two-hour lunch period. But since both parents are working, she has no one at home to greet her. She's also on her own when school lets out at four.

Usually, retired workers, like this woman, run the neighbor-hood committees.

"Children can get into a great deal of trouble without supervision," Old Auntie Lao tells the other committee members, remembering Tiyi. "We're already running a preschool day-care center. Why don't we expand to care for the older children as well?"

So the committee starts preparing food to serve the schoolchildren when they come home at noon, charging the parents only a few pennies. Afterward, the committee supervises the children and sees that they get a rest period before it's time to go back to school.

After school, the committee turns the community hall with its television set over to the youngsters to watch a children's program. Sometimes the program is on elementary science. Sometimes it is about geography or history. The programs always close with a cartoon showing the way good Communist children should behave.

When the television show is over, the children bring out their homework and do it under the supervision of a retired worker who has been through high school. By the time their parents come home, the young students have finished their lessons and the evenings are free.

Mr. Wang is the favorite cook in Meiling's household. When he announces the meal is ready, the family lines up. One by one they fill their bowls and take them outside to eat because it's too hot and stuffy inside. The parents bring out chairs to sit on. The children perch on the door stoop or a low retaining wall. The clack of chopsticks and smacking of lips tell father Wang how much his cooking is appreciated.

This is a pleasant time of day. Late afternoon sunlight is touching only the tops of the buildings, and a light breath of air from the river is stirring in the lanes. All around the Wangs, neighbors have come out to eat their supper in the cool of the day.

A family prepares for an evening meal, which the mother is bringing out from the kitchen. Eating outdoors is a common sight on warm summer nights.

Two solemn-faced six-year-old boys have hurried through their meal to get in a game of cards. Seated on small chairs in front of a little table, they survey their hands. Old Auntie Lao is through with her meal too. Now she is knitting away on a half-finished sweater. She intends to send it to her oldest grandson, who is in the army, stationed in the cold Northeast Region.

Suddenly the homey atmosphere is shattered by violent shouts and the clatter of kettles being thrown around. Two little boys dash out of a doorway and run shrieking to Old Auntie Lao.

"Auntie, Auntie, mother and father are fighting. They're going to kill each other," the boys scream, flinging themselves on Old Auntie Lao.

Sighing, Auntie Lao puts aside her knitting and gets to her feet, because a part of her responsibility is to mediate disputes. With a child clinging to either hand, she walks to the door from which the shouts are issuing. A short while later, the clamor dies down and then stops altogether. Quiet settles again on the neighborhood. Auntie Lao comes out and goes back to her knitting.

Auntie Lao feels that smoothing out marital quarrels in the beginning is very important. It keeps ill feeling from growing and growing until things end in the divorce court. Of course if people are really incompatible, divorce is the only answer, and the courts recognize this. But first, serious attempts at reconciliation must be made by different mediating parties—the neighborhood committee, the factory committee, and finally, if things go that far, a committee appointed by the divorce court.

Sometimes Auntie Lao has to settle disputes between neighbors, such as the time Wei Fang, the carpenter, started to build an addition to his kitchen without realizing he was blocking off the sunlight from his neighbor's windows. That problem took some adroit replanning, but in the end Wei Fang had a larger kitchen and his neighbor had her sunlight.

One of the chief causes of dissension in Chinese cities is overcrowding because of the housing shortage. Auntie Lao knows that in the old days all the relatives—aunts, uncles, and grandparents—lived together in a sprawling complex, sharing courtyards and kitchens. But this arrangement didn't make for harmony.

Today the government is trying to solve the problem by providing more housing. It believes it's better for the older people to have their own apartments and just visit their children from time to time. Once they get used to the idea, the grandparents like this too. Most of them are retirees living on pensions that amount to from 60 to 100 percent of their salaries.

However there are some elderly people, usually women, who never had the opportunity to work and so get no pension. They receive a small stipend from the government, and their working children are expected to provide for the rest of their needs. Sometimes young couples don't want to be bothered. Then Old Auntie Lao has to explain to them that this is the law and that there are penalties for disobeying it.

Evening meal over, the adults in the neighborhood start gathering in the community hall. Here, twice a week, Old Auntie Lao and her committee members chair political study sessions. The sessions are spent discussing ways of furthering the Four Modernizations in the community and of improving the spiritual quality of life by thinking more of others and of the country than of oneself.

Committee members also use the sessions to explain newly enacted laws to the neighborhood people. These laws have in turn been explained to them by government representatives. Tonight a meeting has been called to launch one of the neighborhood's periodic campaigns on hygiene. The audience hears a lecture about the many illnesses that are caused by germs which breed in filth. The lecture ends with a rallying call to clean up homes and neighborhood. During the following weeks, committee members will go around inspecting households, work places, schools, and restaurants to check on sanitary conditions.

Physical well-being is a special concern of the committee. It runs a small neighborhood clinic with a staff that has been trained by doctors to diagnose illnesses and treat the simple ones. The staff members also know how to give children preventive inoculations against such diseases as diphtheria, whooping cough, tetanus, tuberculosis, polio, and measles.

There is a health clinic in every neighborhood, factory, and government building. Every district has a hospital or big health center. These can handle many of the more serious ailments. Major cases are sent to the large city hospitals.

But the overcrowded, understaffed hospitals often make it difficult to help patients who have mental and emotional rather than physical ailments. Statistics show that in the city of Shanghai alone, almost eight people in every thousand are suffering some kind of mental or emotional illness. Four in every thousand have been diagnosed as schizophrenics, or people with personality disorders. Yet the city has only 328 doctors to take care of such patients. One hundred and four of them are highly qualified. The rest are medics. There are only 822 nurses in the field and 5,838 hospital beds for such patients. This means that most people who are mentally or emotionally ill must be treated at home by volunteers or members of their families. In cities such as Shanghai, where some help is available, the volunteers are aided by hospital doctors to whom they make regular reports. Once or twice a week the patients are brought in for treatment.

Meiling and Shaoli, who have no television set at home, often enjoy an evening watching programs in the community hall. The community television set is available to everyone. And though more and more people are saving their money to buy their own sets, the rest still prefer to spend their savings on other items.

The programs always begin with a newscast. This is followed by televised sports events or a travelogue on some scenic spot in China, or a documentary on the customs and life-style of another country. Occasionally there is a live show put on by Shanghai's own performing arts troupe, which is made up of 130 persons. It may be a filmed Chinese opera, a historical drama, or a comedy.

Watching television isn't the young women's only entertainment.

Sometimes they go out for a meal on the town. There are a few fashionable government-run restaurants in Shanghai. Here gourmet dinners are served by efficient uniformed waiters. But though the meals are not really expensive by American standards, they're much more than Meiling and Shaoli can afford. Instead they visit a popular family-run restaurant located on an upper floor of an old building. The grimy stairs leading to it are dimly lit, but the room itself is bathed in bright light streaming from bare bulbs hanging from the ceiling.

Most of the patrons sitting around the rough tables are young people. They are either studying menus or eating with gusto. There's a lot of boisterous laughter at a table where China's famous Tsingtao beer is being served.

The waiters, wearing spotted aprons, rush about banging down big bowls of noodle and vegetable soup, fried shrimp, pork or fish dishes, and rice in front of their customers. The dishes are wholesome and

This is a gourmet restaurant. The surroundings are plain, but the food is not. Only those with high salaries can afford to come here.

very cheap. But the service is not the best. Sometimes a wrong dish is served or a dish doesn't meet with a customer's approval. Then an angry voice is raised in complaint. The waiter, uncowed, replies in kind. The patron bangs the table with his fist and shouts out a string of epithets. The waiter furiously orders him to be quiet. The room rocks with laughter. But soon things settle down again.

Sometimes Meiling and Shaoli go to a movie house to catch a film they've heard about. It costs them only a few fen. Taking along pumpkin and sunflower seeds in their pockets for a snack, they sit through the picture cracking and munching away. They offend no one because everybody else is snacking too. By the time the picture is over, the floor of the theater is littered with seed shells and candy wrappers.

Sometimes a troupe of touring performers puts on a live show— a ballet, an opera, or acrobatics. Then the Wang family may go to see it together. The shows begin early and let out in time for families to get home before the children's bedtime. Meiling's sister, Holai, always enjoys these outings.

One night a magician on tour comes to the city to put on a magic show. Holai sits on the edge of her seat, her eyes huge. She gasps wonderingly every time the magician miraculously extracts doves, rabbits, colored scarves from hats, small boxes from his sleeves.

During intermission the theater buzzes with conversation. Children wriggle in their seats, hungrily eyeing the little refreshment carts that theater attendants are wheeling up and down the aisles. Holai shivers with eagerness as her father stops the cart on its way up the aisle. He reaches in his pocket for money to buy the whole family ice-cream bars on sticks.

Settling back in her chair, Holai munches on the ice cream. The lights dim. The magician returns. Holai catches her breath in excitement. Meiling is stirred by the same thrill of anticipation her little sister feels. Banished to a poor isolated region for so many years, she was deprived of most entertainment. Now she is thirsty for all the big city has to offer.

The Wedding

Meiling and Shaoli are worried about ever finding a husband. Already they are past the marriageable age, which is twenty-two for women and twenty-three for men. Marriage is still very important to young as well as older people in China, where the family has traditionally been the center of life. There are few single persons. And since couples who marry do so with the intention of spending the rest of their lives together, finding the right partner is a very serious matter.

Meiling and Shaoli's problem is that in their job they don't come into contact with young men. And outside of events in places of work, there is very little social activity in the city. So it's difficult to meet members of the opposite sex.

In the old days, marriages were arranged by matchmakers who worked with the parents to bring together two young people. Before their wedding day, the bride and groom had usually never laid eyes on each other. Some women were fortunate in the men their families picked for them. But often such blind matchmaking resulted in tragic marriages that occasionally ended in suicide for the brides.

Today young people are free to choose their own mates. But the problem of getting suitable couples together remains. Sometimes a friend or relative plays the part of matchmaker by introducing young people to each other. But this doesn't always happen.

Meiling and Shaoli have decided to turn to a volunteer matchmaking service that has just opened in the city. It is called Bridge for Young People and is run by the Communist Youth League to help young men and women meet each other in social surroundings.

It takes Meiling and Shaoli a while to find the courage to go to the Bridge for Young People office. But at last, one evening after supper they set out on their adventure. And they discover it's not so difficult after all. They're put at ease at once by the young woman volunteer at the reception desk. She greets them pleasantly and asks if they're looking for suitable mates. Blushing, Meiling and Shaoli nod their heads.

The clerk asks to see their identification cards, then hands each one a form to fill out. The form asks for such information as age, occupation, income, health, and level of education. When the forms are completed, Meiling and Shaoli turn them in.

"We always check into people's background," the volunteer tells them, taking their forms. "If we find they're good citizens and aren't already going steady with anyone and have no serious arrest record, we'll try to match them up with someone they'll find compatible."

She gestures toward her files.

"Everyone in there has been thoroughly investigated and has been found to be very respectable," she tells them. "We'll surely be able to find someone who will suit you. We'll contact you in a few days."

True to her word, the next evening the clerk calls Meiling and Shaoli on the neighborhood phone.

"I have two young men for you to meet," she says. "They'll be here tomorrow night. Can you come?"

The next evening finds Meiling and Shaoli again in the office of the Bridge for Young People. Two young men are waiting awkwardly by the clerk's desk. They are dock workers and have had very little opportunity to meet women. The clerk introduces them and then leads them to a small reception room where there are several easy chairs. Hot water in a thermos bottle and a dish of pumpkin seeds make up the refreshments.

The clerk hands the young women's files to the men and the men's files to the women. Then she sits down unobtrusively in a corner of the room. The couples study the files. Presently they begin to exchange a little timid conversation. The clerk comes over and pours hot water in teacups and serves the pumpkin seeds. She tells them that she is arranging a party for newly acquainted couples like themselves. It will be held in this office. Perhaps they would like to come too.

The newly introduced couples look uneasy. They have never been to a large social event before, they tell the clerk. They are used to their neighborhood friends. How will they behave with strangers?

The clerk laughs. "Everyone else will be feeling the same way," she assures the two couples. "But you will find it will be fun."

Meiling and Shaoli and the young dock workers attend the party. It's a simple affair. The other couples who arrive at the office reception room are all embarrassed too. They don't know exactly how to behave in a social situation. Everyone blushes a lot. Hardly a word is spoken.

Only the smiling young clerk and her fiancé, who has come with her, seem at ease. They serve tea and little cakes and start a conversation. One by one the other couples are drawn into it. Someone tells a joke. The others start laughing.

As the evening progresses, the couples loosen up. Chatter mingled with laughter fills the room. By nine o'clock, when the party is ready to break up, all the partners seem to be on good terms with each other. The clerk serves refreshments, ladling out bowls of sweet congee, a kind of gruel made of rice and tiny beans mixed with sugar.

By this time Meiling and Shaoli and the young men are feeling quite comfortable together. On one of their days off, the two men invite the young women to the docks where they work. Here they watch long-armed cranes load and unload tons of rolled steel, steel tubing, sacks of grain, bales of yarn and silk. Wharf trucks rumble along carrying goods to ship or storehouse. Everywhere there's excitement and bustle.

On another of their days off, the young men come to the snack bar in the park and stay to visit during the slack periods. Then the four begin going out together on regular dates—to live shows, to movies, and to sports events. Perhaps as they get to know each other better, they will find they are not really suited. Then they will go back to the Bridge for Young People and ask the clerk to find someone else. If they decide on marriage, the service will arrange a simple wedding reception for them and even help them to buy the furniture they need to set up house.

Meiling's older brother Daming has had no problem meeting young women in his job as one of the managers in a state department store. For three years he has been going with a young clerk named Baihua. They've been planning marriage for some time. But they've waited until they could save enough money to buy their own furniture, including a large television set, for the new apartment they'll be renting near their place of work.

The couple hasn't even thought of signing up for one of the houses which the government has begun to build recently to ease the housing shortage. Individuals can either buy these houses outright or take out government mortgages at low—1 to 2 percent—interest. If people are able to build their own homes, the government will provide them with free materials.

But Daming is no carpenter. And he and Baihua want to avoid going into debt. Auntie Lao is pleased with the young couple's thrifty outlook. It's proof that the lectures she and her committee have been giving against extravagant weddings are taking effect. These lectures are part of a nationwide campaign by the government. It includes coverage by television, radio, and newspapers on

A typical apartment kitchen that must be shared by several families, because of the severe housing shortage in China.

what is called the old feudal practice of bartering away the bride.

The campaign was launched when it was discovered that more and more young women and their families were beginning to demand all kinds of expensive gifts from the fiancé when a couple became engaged. Some young women even refused to set the wedding date until they had these gifts, which might range from full sets of furniture to television sets, sewing machines, bicycles, and watches.

The wedding reception can be another big expense. In China it is the bridegroom's family that is responsible for it. Some families are so afraid of losing face with the bride's relations that they arrange feasts to which as many as 300 guests may be invited. In the end, parents, along with the newlyweds, are thousands of yuan in debt. Usually this happens just before retirement age, when the parents should be looking forward to a life free of harassment.

Daming and Baihua have decided against a big wedding feast. Instead, they will have a simple reception in the lounge of their department store. Their fellow employees decorate the room, while Daming's mother and sisters prepare the refreshments. They have bought bulk candy, which they put in small plastic bags that are printed with the character "double happiness" in red. The bags will be handed out to the guests as mementos.

Meanwhile, Daming and Baihua go to the marriage registration office for their certificates. Once they receive these certificates, they will be considered legally married. On the threshold of the office, Baihua hangs back bashfully and Daming has to urge her inside.

A middle-aged clerk comes forward to greet them. Her manner is so motherly that Baihua is soon at ease. Daming hands the clerk the letter he has brought from the committee of his department store. It informs the clerk that the backgrounds of Daming and Baihua have been carefully investigated, that neither of them is secretly married, and both are of legal marriage age.

After the clerk reads the letter, she invites the couple to sit down. Then she asks Daming to give his name, his age, and his nationality. She asks for the same information from Baihua. Next she wants to know how they became acquainted and how long they have been going together. She asks what their parents think about the marriage.

"Were you free to choose each other, or have you been pressured into this marriage by relatives?" she inquires searchingly.

When the couple answers all her questions satisfactorily, the clerk explains the recently passed marriage laws to them. She tells Daming that the law requires that he consider Baihua his equal in every way.

She tells Baihua she may retain her maiden name after her marriage if she chooses. And the couple's children will be free to adopt whichever surname they please.

Working couples, she continues, must share the responsibility for family expenditures, household chores, and the raising of children. The wife has as much right to own property as the husband. If either dies before the other, the survivor inherits the property of the deceased.

The clerk then goes on to the subject of children. She explains that census figures show China has surpassed the billion mark in population. Something must be done to stop this rapid growth, or the whole country will face starvation.

"We must not only keep from expanding but should try to roll back if possible," she tells the young people. "That's why we're asking every couple to limit their family to one child. You can get contraceptive devices or birth control pills free in your community. If you find yourself pregnant and wish to get an abortion, you can have one without cost at your local hospital. If after the first child, Baihua wants to have her tubes tied or you, Daming, want a vasectomy, the operation will be performed for you free."

At this point, the clerk hands the couple a sheet of paper on which a pledge to have only one child is printed.

"The government is so concerned about the overpopulation problem, it is rewarding every couple that signs this pledge," the clerk explains. "When the child is born, the couple will be given an honor certificate which will entitle them to an annual bonus equal to two months' salary of one of them. Their child may go to school tuition free and will receive special medical care and treatment without charge. That child will be given preference in job placement also. But let me warn you, if the pledge is broken and a second child comes along, the couple will lose those benefits. If a third child arrives, they will be docked 10 percent of their income."

Daming and Baihua have heard all this information many times from their neighborhood committee. They willingly sign the pledge.

Then the clerk hands them each a signed marriage certificate. Beaming, she congratulates them and wishes them a long and worthwhile life.

Daming and Baihua set off for the department store. They step shyly through the doorway of the lounge and look around at the transformed room. An 8 by 10 portrait of the bride and groom hangs on one wall, beside a picture of a pine tree and a blossoming plum branch, painted by Meiling. The plum is the symbol for happiness and good fortune. The pine tree stands for everlasting faithfulness through summer and winter alike. Another wall is plastered with two huge red paper cutouts of the character "double happiness." Guests are seated about, and plates of food and cups of tea have been set out.

In front of the blue drapes hanging across one end of the room, stands the master of ceremonies, microphone in hand. He is a fellow worker and Daming's best friend. The guests burst into applause as Daming and Baihua appear. The master of ceremonies goes over to them and ushers them to the microphone.

"Now you must tell us the story of how you met and fell in love," he says.

Daming and Baihua blush and stand there tongue-tied. The guests laugh.

"Then I will have to do it myself," the master of ceremonies announces. He leads the couple to two chairs set in the place of honor before the blue drapes.

When Daming and Baihua are seated, the master of ceremonies begins to recite the ballad he has written. Step by step in lengthy detail, the ballad describes the progress the young couple made from their first meeting to this wedding day. Some of the older people are in tears as they listen to the story of the young couple's love, told in the sentimental fashion of a modern fairy tale. The eyes of the unmarried young people glisten with the hope that one day such good fortune may befall them too.

When the ballad comes to an end, friends and relatives congratu-

This peasant woman is being urged not to have more children, because China's population is over one billion. Since her child is a boy, she may be satisfied, although peasants traditionally want large families.

late the young couple and admire their marriage certificates. Daming and Baihua present each guest with one of the small candy bags. And the reception comes to an end.

But the bride and groom still have a treat before them. The Shanghai Travel Service has decided to give a reward to several young couples who have been content with modest wedding ceremonies. Daming and Baihua are among the lucky couples chosen. Tomorrow they will set out by train for a three-day honeymoon in the lovely southern city of Hangzhou, once the summer retreat of emperors.

The young couple will be put up in a hostel and spend their days sight-seeing, taking boat rides on the lake, drinking tea, and eating sweets in the pavilions of Hangzhou's many islands. And at night they will see the great moon rise over the wooded slopes of the mountains and hear the chirping of thousands of crickets—symbols of contentment and happiness from ancient times.

Earthquake

Liu Baolang is in her last year of senior middle school. She lives in an orphanage outside the mining city of Tangshan. She was ten when she lost her parents. Sometimes she has nightmares about it. Then she seems to hear her parents and her little sisters screaming for help.

It happened the night of July 28, 1975. At three in the morning an earthquake hit the city of some million inhabitants. Tangshan is built over an earthquake fault. There are a number of such faults in China, running in parallel courses north to south. Some are in the far west. Others lie in the coastal region.

Through the centuries there have been periodic earthquakes along these fault lines. But the Tangshan earthquake was China's worst on record. The epicenter of the tremor, which measured 7.5 on the Richter scale, was located directly under the city. It was so violent that Beijing, which is about one hundred miles west of Tangshan, also suffered severe damage.

Baolang, who lived in a small adobe house with her parents and two younger sisters, was jolted out of a deep sleep when the earth under her started to rumble and then to heave like the sea. In the jet blackness that enveloped her, Baolang could hear chunks of ceiling and heavy rafters falling with a crash all around her. One rafter, wedged slantwise over her bed, prevented other debris from crushing her. But across the room she could hear the screams of her sisters, and farther away the cries of her parents.

Baolang tried to clamber out of bed, but she couldn't move until the first tremor stopped. Then she was able to sit up, only to bang her head against the rafter. She tried to push past it to reach her screaming sisters, but an aftershock almost as severe as the initial quake threw her back on her bed. She lay there terrified, while shocks kept coming one and two minutes apart.

With each shock, Baolang heard the crash of more debris falling. Her family's screams faded away as the house settled. Then suddenly the side of the room by her bed fell outward, leaving a block of black sky. Baolang crept into the open and began stumbling aimlessly about, looking for help.

All around her, the earth kept quaking and heaving. Houses and four-story apartment buildings had all been turned into great heaps of rubble. Screams and groans from the midst of the rubble filled the air. Shadowy figures were running to and fro with flashlights.

Baolang snatched at the figures to ask them to help her family, but no one noticed her. Their thoughts were on rescuing those who could still be heard screaming from the debris.

Baolang wandered forlornly on. Then a child's wail caught her attention. In the first pale glimmering of dawn, she saw that it was a small boy. A steel girder had fallen across both his legs, crushing them. Baolang knelt beside him. There was nothing she could do to free him, but she put her arms around him and tried to comfort him. His sobbing stopped. He whimpered a little and then was still. He had died in Baolang's arms, but she thought he was only sleeping. She sat there dazed, clinging to him.

Around her the day brightened. Rescue work was being organized.

News of the disaster had been sent out by a telegraph operator. From the nearest airfields, planes of the People's Liberation Army began to fly overhead, dropping food and clothing. Trucks followed, bringing in bottled water, for the tremors had burst the city mains and all drinking water was dangerously polluted. Soldiers came, bringing picks and shovels to help dig out those buried in the rubble. And 40,000 medical workers from various cities began arriving.

A young woman paramedic found Baolang still sitting in a corner of debris holding the dead child tightly. The woman knelt by the dazed girl and gently pried her arms from the boy's corpse. She picked up Baolang and carried her to one of the tents the soldiers had set up for wounded survivors. Realizing the child was in shock, the woman wrapped her in quilts, poured hot tea into a cup, and held it to the girl's lips, speaking comfortingly all the while.

On all sides, there was the bustle of medical workers accompanied by the groans of the injured who were being brought here on makeshift stretchers. After being given first aid, the more serious cases were flown to hospitals in other cities. Meanwhile all survivors were inoculated to guard against possible epidemics of cholera, typhoid, or diphtheria.

By 3 P.M., city residents and soldiers had formed into teams which began a systematic search for survivors and bodies. As they worked, another strong shock caused the debris of the ruined city to settle even further. A heavy rain began to fall.

Operations had to wait until morning. Then rescue attempts began again. Much of the heartbreaking work was identifying the already decomposing corpses. Orphaned children were gathered together in some of the tents, where they were cared for by volunteer workers. Many like Baolang were dazed with shock. Others couldn't stop screaming. There were 2,700 such children in all. Others had lost only one parent. Eight thousand wives and 7,000 husbands had been made widows and widowers. Whole families had been wiped out, including children, parents, and grandparents, along with other relatives. Altogether some 148,000 people had died. Surprisingly, scarcely any lives were lost among the miners on the night shift, though they had been underground at the time. A geological quirk had kept the tunnels in which they had been working from caving in.

Large as the casualty figures were, they would have been much worse in the old days. Quick relief was unheard of then, and people starved by the millions after such natural disasters. But modern China is able to mobilize her forces and supplies quickly. Soon teams of workers began arriving from all over the province to clear away the rubble and rebuild the city.

Many of the orphans had surviving relatives who took them in. The others, Baolang among them, were placed in an orphanage built for them. Baolang has lived there ever since. When the children first arrived at the orphanage, they were bewildered and frightened. Many kept crying for their parents. Others sat silent for hours, even refusing to eat. When heavy thunderstorms struck, they would all scurry outdoors, screaming in terror, thinking that the roll of thunder was another earthquake.

The city was restored rapidly. Water was pumped out of the mine tunnels, and miners went back to work. The ceramics factory, where Baolang's parents had been employed, reopened. New apartment buildings, reenforced against earthquakes, rose on the old sites. A sanitarium was built for the city's 1,700 paraplegics, crippled by the quake. All suffered various degrees of paralysis, from severed to badly torn spinal cords. The city's population swelled. In a few years it had surpassed its former million mark.

Seven years have gone by, but Baolang has not forgotten the kindness of the young paramedic who treated her for shock that terrible day, and now she wants to be a doctor herself. There are obstacles in her way, however, as institutions of higher learning are limited in China. There are less than 700 colleges and universities to accommodate all the young people clamoring for admission. These institutions cover all fields: liberal arts, teacher training, technology, science, and medicine. Their total enrollment is around

A high school student puts what he has learned in class to the test in a school workshop. Schools in China mix theory with practice.

1,020,000 students, so those who want to get in have to score the highest marks in stiff entrance examinations.

The examinations are prepared by professors selected by the government. They convene in Beijing to prepare the questions along with the standard answers. After the examination questions have been prepared, the professors are sent to a summer resort where they live in isolation until the examinations have been given. This is to prevent any leakage.

The examinations start on the same day at the same hour all over the country. Since China does not measure time by zones, six o'clock in Beijing is also six o'clock in far distant Xinjiang (Sinkiang), a thousand miles away. Newspapers announce the date of the examinations, which fall in two general categories—liberal arts and science.

The examinations for liberal arts consist of questions on history, geography, foreign language, politics, and Chinese language and literature. For science, the questions are concerned with medicine, mathematics, chemistry, physics, Chinese language and literature, politics, and a foreign language—either English, Japanese, German, French, Russian, Spanish, or Arabic.

Examination time is a harrowing experience for all the contestants, who know that only the top 4 percent of the applicants will be accepted. To make sure that this 4 percent is fairly chosen, every student is given a number, and the number is coded against the name. Professors who grade the papers know the students only by number. Later, numbers are matched to names, and those who qualify receive letters.

Baolang gets a letter. She has qualified and has been chosen by the Beijing Medical College. She will live in a dormitory on the school campus. The government takes care of all the expenses of subsidized students except food. But because Baolang is an orphan, she will be given a small monthly allowance to cover this need too. Baolang does not need to worry about getting a position after she graduates, as China is short of doctors.

Baolang is fortunate. Two years ago her good friend Shanmin, who grew up in the orphanage with her, wanted a degree in education so she could become a qualified high school teacher. But even though her marks were excellent, they were not quite high enough for her to get into the government's subsidized program.

Some of the high-scoring young people who do not qualify for the government program still have a chance to continue their education. Several universities and colleges have begun enrolling additional students on a self-paying basis. Their tuition runs from 20 to 25 yuan (10 to 12½ American dollars) each term. They live at home and work during the day, attending school at night when the university's facilities and professors are available. Upon graduation they are given certificates. More and more high schools are also being used for night classes.

Unfortunately, no night schools have opened in Tangshan yet. But Shanmin had another opportunity to complete her studies. The Central Broadcasting and Television Station in Beijing holds classes over the air for students across the country. The television school teaches eighteen basic and specialized courses. Teachers from a number of key universities give televised lectures.

Shanmin was able to get a daytime job in the ceramics factory and enroll in the television school. It was a tough grind for her. She had to buy her own textbooks and other materials, and she had to spend long hours studying at night. Fortunately, the courses she took had to do with liberal arts rather than science, which, without a laboratory in which to experiment, is much more difficult to learn.

Just this year, Shanmin completed the necessary courses and passed the examinations. She was granted a certificate and assigned to teach in a middle school in Harbin, capital of China's northernmost Heilungjiang province in the Northeast Region. Baolang and the rest of the orphanage family saw her off early this summer.

There's another big celebration in the orphanage to honor Baolang's good fortune. Workers at the ceramics factory where her parents were employed purchase new clothes for her and give her a small gift of money. Then after a routine physical checkup at the local hospital, Baolang boards the train for the capital.

Women Hold Up
Half the Sky

Baolang's train runs through a flat plain cultivated with wheat, a prosperous looking land dotted here and there by clusters of adobe villages sheltered under copses of trees. Autumn has yellowed the wheat, and already the reaping has started. Much of it is being done with scythes in the old-fashioned way. But here and there, a few large red harvesters, along with tractors, are at work. On a distant road, Baolang notices some trucks in the procession of horse-drawn carts. Mechanization is coming only gradually to China's farmlands.

All the wide, flat expanse of yellow earth that stretches to the horizon as far as Baolang can see is the work of the Yellow River. For many millions of years it has been carrying heavy loads of silt from the western uplands to dump them here, until it built up some 200,000 square miles of land. Today this land is known as the Yellow River Plain or the North China Plain.

Baolang turns from the window to look into the strong, lined face

This north China village is typical of the villages that dot the Yellow River Plain.

and earnest dark eyes of the woman sitting next to her. She recognizes the woman. It's Mrs. Luan Pingyuan, a representative of the National Federation of Women. She's just been to Tangshan to hold discussions on women's rights.

Mrs. Luan has a natural curiosity about people, especially where young women are concerned. And it isn't long before the sixty-year-old woman has drawn Baolang out of her shyness. Soon the girl is telling her about the dreadful night of the earthquake. She describes her life in the orphanage and now her unbelievable good fortune in being accepted by Beijing Medical College.

Mrs. Luan smiles at the girl.

"I wonder if you really understand the extent of your good fortune, young lady," she says. "When I was young, we women suffered so much."

Luan Pingyuan lapses into silence as a long ago New Year's Day rises before her eyes. She was only a child at the time, and her parents had taken her visiting at a friend's house. An old woman was sitting in a corner with her feet stretched out in front of her, tiny feet in red shoes no more than three inches long.

The shoes were the only elegant thing about the woman. She was wearing faded trousers and a grimy jacket, while the rest of the household was in holiday finery. Everyone was exchanging New Year's greetings, laughing and talking, passing around sweets. But no one was taking any notice of the old woman. And she was paying no attention to them. She just sat crouched with her head bent, pulling stitches out of a tattered padded jacket to save the cotton stuffing inside.

Afterward, Pingyuan had asked her mother why the old woman was being treated that way. And her mother had answered, "Because she's bad luck. You shouldn't have noticed her either."

Her mother had gone on to explain that when the woman was very young, she was so beautiful, her parents had no trouble finding a rich husband for her. She was considered especially desirable because of her tiny feet, which the Chinese men called Golden Lilies.

Golden Lily feet were the fashion when the old woman was young. No respectable man would marry a girl whose feet weren't bound. So when a girl was just five years old or so, her mother started wrapping strips of wet cotton cloth around her feet. As the cloth dried, it shrank, squeezing the heel and the ball of the foot together and crushing the bone with the toes underneath. Every day the mother would tighten the bindings. The pain was so terrible that the little girl would cry all night, but she had to keep the bandages on, because without tiny feet she couldn't get a husband. And unmarried girls were considered a disgrace in old China.

By the time little girls were eleven or twelve, the binding stopped. By this time they had been turned into cripples. With feet only three inches long and shaped like goats' hooves they could hardly hobble around. But their feet were now able to fit into the tiny red satin shoes with high heels which the men considered so elegant.

Foot-binding had been going on for centuries. What attraction did the men see in such feet? No one really knew. Some people said they wanted the women to have feet as small as those of a famous court dancer who lived long ago. Others said that the tiny crushed feet and the hip-swaying walk that they caused aroused the men sexually. And still others were sure it was that men found the bound feet a sure way to keep their wives from running off, no matter how badly they were treated at home. With bound feet, they were too crippled to get around except by hobbling. Rich women were carried from place to place by attendants. Poor peasant girls often had to do heavy household chores by crawling around on their hands and knees.

Pingyuan's mother had gone on to explain the cause for the old woman's bad fortune. Her own household had been well-to-do. But go-betweens had arranged a marriage for her with an even wealthier family. She had never met her bridegroom until her wedding day, when she was borne to her new home in a scarlet sedan chair. A red carpet was spread before her, and she was carried over it into the house on the backs of attendants. From then on she was waited on by servants. The only thing expected of her was to bear a son.

But she had borne no son, and misfortune had struck her husband's family. They lost much of their money through unwise investments and blamed the young woman for bringing them bad luck. They threw her out of the house.

Her sister took her in because it would have been a disgrace on the family name to leave her without shelter. For more than fifty years, she lived in her sister's home as a slave. She did menial chores around the place, wore clothes that were almost in tatters, and ate leftovers from the table after the others were finished. During all that time, no one spoke to her. How had she endured those long lonely years?

Sitting here in the train beside this pretty young girl with such a bright future before her, Luan Pingyuan's memories engulf her with pain. Baolang becomes aware of the grief in the strong face turned to her.

"What are you thinking of, Auntie?" she asks, breaking into the older woman's reverie.

"I'm thinking of all the little girls who had to suffer bound feet in the past," Mrs. Luan answers. "Do you know, young lady, sometimes those children died of blood poisoning? Sometimes their feet just rotted off. Those that lived were crippled for the rest of their lives. And what for? For nothing!"

Baolang shudders, looking at Luan Pingyuan's feet.

Luan Pingyuan laughs. "I was fortunate," she tells the girl. "Even my mother escaped. Grandmother had just begun binding my mother's feet when Dr. Sun Yat-sen overthrew the Manchus and started his republic. Dr. Sun hated foot-binding. He'd seen the suffering his little sister had to go through when his mother insisted on binding her feet. He tried to make her stop, but he was only thirteen, and she wouldn't listen to him.

"When Dr. Sun grew up, he campaigned against foot-binding. And his wife, Soong Ching Ling, joined him. She didn't have bound feet. Her father had sent her and her two sisters to America to get a Western education. She and a few others worked hard for women's rights from the beginning.

"The campaign against foot-binding was very successful in the coastal cities. My grandmother was caught up in the new spirit of the times, and my mother's bandages came off before any real damage was done. But in the back country, people went right on binding feet until the People's Republic was founded in 1949. Then foot-binding was stopped everywhere."

"I'm glad, Auntie. It must have been terrible," Baolang says.

"Women didn't suffer just from foot-binding," Pingyuan continues. "They were bound in other ways too. All their lives they were bound—first by their fathers and brothers, then by their husbands and mothers-in-law. Can you believe that in some places they weren't addressed by their own names until they were seventy years old? Then they were given their names at a great celebration to honor their age—nothing else. They were considered of so little account that they went by nicknames when they were little. After they were married, they were referred to as the person in so-and-so's family.

"When a young girl was married and went to her new husband's home, she found herself under the complete control of her husband and mother-in-law. The mother-in-law often treated the newcomer like a slave. You see, she had the right to scold and beat her, to make her work from morning to night. The only way a young wife could save herself was to bear a son. Then she would be given more respect. When she became a mother-in-law herself, she frequently took out all her early sufferings on the brides that married her sons."

Baolang stares at Luan Pingyuan. "But Auntie, mothers-in-law aren't allowed to do that now," she points out.

The older woman nods and her voice grows gentle as she continues. "Young lady, when you were orphaned by the Tangshan earthquake, do you realize how fortunate you were to have had a home to stay in all those years? In the old days you would have become a beggar, or perhaps someone would have taken you off to be a slave in a city factory or a prostitute in a brothel. No one would have cared a bit about you because you're a girl. Boys, though, would have been quickly adopted into families that had no sons.

"Whenever there were famines, poor parents kept their boy children and sold their girl children. Often the girls were bought by older men who were already married. These girls became second wives, or concubines. But they were usually slaves to the first wife and were often treated cruelly by her. In those early days, suicide was the only defense women had against the cruelties practiced on them.

"Then there were the poor girls who were sometimes betrothed at birth to much older men. If the man died before the girl reached marriageable age, she might be forced to be the bride in a symbolic wedding, with a tablet or a rooster representing the dead man. After this she was regarded as a widow, and widows were not permitted to remarry.

"That's why so many women joined Dr. Sun Yat-sen's revolution. He promised them equality in his new republic. Many women joined

Mao Zedong and the Communist Party in the civil war and the war against Japan for the same reason. They fought as valiantly as any man. Mao Zedong was so impressed by their bravery that he, too, promised them equality once the new government was founded."

Baolang nods. She has heard all this before at school, but now as the older woman talks, it comes alive for her.

"And you, Auntie?" she asks, leaning toward the woman.

"I was fortunate compared to many others," Luan Pingyuan answers. "My family was well-to-do, and they loved me. But they never believed I was the equal of my brothers. Most girls weren't sent to school as their brothers were. If they got any education at all, it was at home under tutors. My father got me a good tutor. I was educated. But I wasn't allowed to leave my home or hunt for work."

"But you married," Baolang says.

"Yes, my parents found a husband for me. Fortunately he was a kind man and his mother welcomed me. But they wouldn't let me live a life of my own.

"After the People's Republic of China was founded, government representatives were sent everywhere to explain the new laws that made women equal to men. Women were told it wasn't enough for the government to pass laws to give them equality. They would have to fight for their rights themselves. The government promised to back them.

"So the women formed the National Federation of Women. I joined it too, even though my husband objected at first. Now I'm a representative, meeting with women everywhere. I tell them to unite and stand up for their right to equal pay for equal jobs, the right to be engineers, doctors, or scientists if they have the talent for it. I dreamed of being an engineer, I wanted to get out into the world, not stay at home all day. You are doing what I always wanted to do. The young women of today have that chance."

Until now, Baolang hasn't given much thought to the great strides that Chinese women have made in the past thirty years. She knows there is still discrimination. Shanmin, for instance, got only three-fourths of the pay that men working in her shop received. And she's aware that women are still being passed over in promotions, that they're still holding very few high political posts. It is only someone of Luan Pingyuan's years who can look back to see the great progress women have already made.

"Never forget our slogan, young lady," Mrs. Luan says. "Women Hold Up Half the Sky. See that you hold up your half."

"I'll do my best, Auntie," Baolang promises.

Baolang is one of an increasing number of young women who are passing examinations with higher marks than men. In some medical universities, 50 percent of the students are young women, and the professors are glad to have them because they are so dedicated. A large number of these female students, like Baolang, are interested in surgery. And many of their instructors in this field are women too.

Wherever women have been given a chance, they are excelling. One-third of the 400,000 or so scientists and engineers in China are

Doctors are still in short supply in China, but the government is stepping up medical education to take care of the lack.

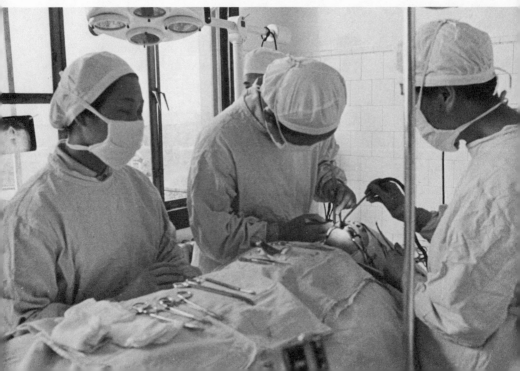

women. Some have attained outstanding achievements. He Zehui, a researcher at the High Energy Physics Institute, received China's Academy of Sciences Award in 1956 and is now working on cosmic ray research.

Baolang hopes she will be worthy of the trust the government is putting in her and become a fine doctor one day. At present, though, she has a whole new life to which she must adjust. Ahead of her lie six years of arduous study. During this time she will share a cramped dormitory room with two other students. The room has three small cots and three small tables. On each table stands a pitcher and washbasin. A hand towel hangs on a rack above them. The students do their laundering and showering down the hall in communal rooms.

A damp chill pervades the whole dormitory in the winter. The floors are cement and the small heaters in the rooms do little to take out the chill. Classrooms are as cold. The students keep warm by putting on layer after layer of sweaters and padded jackets. It isn't easy to study in the cramped dormitory quarters, so most of the students go to the school library and reading rooms, which are always crowded. Students take their meals in the school cafeteria. There food usually consists of noodles or rice, vegetables, and a little meat or fish. The food is not very tasty, but it is cheap.

The students don't complain about their Spartan life or the mediocre food. They know they are fortunate. They are the elite. They will receive not only the best education the university can provide, but the guarantee of a good career in their chosen profession once they have graduated.

Life in the Red Basin

Twenty-four year old Yang Hungniao and her husband Ligong live in a village in the western province of Sichuan. Her home is in the center of the province, the Red Basin, as it is called because of the color of its soil. The landscape around Hungniao's home is a pleasant one, made up of rolling terraced hills and level land over which a patchwork of rice paddies spreads. Ponds dot it, and rivers and irrigation channels lace it.

Sichuan, which means "four rivers," is a well-watered country. The high mountains that hem it in on the north and west block in the summer monsoons that come up from the south, causing most of the rain to fall on Sichuan. The rain averages some forty-five inches a year. The countryside is almost always enveloped in a misty haze from the moisture in the air.

Four main tributaries and many smaller ones stream through the province to join the Yangtze River, which forms part of its southern boundary. Then the great river turns northeast to flow past the city of Chongqing (Chungking) and on down the Three Gorges into eastern China.

Beyond the Three Gorges, the Chinese have built a huge dam, the Gezhou Dam. It is the first step in a giant water control project that will be completed when the Three Gorges complex is built. These two projects will supply China with 30 percent of all the country's hydroelectric power.

Locks on the river will enable freighters of much larger tonnage than at present to pass through the narrow Three Gorges to Chongqing. This is very important because the Yangtze is the country's chief waterway. It carries 80 percent of China's inland water traffic.

Hungniao has never traveled down the mighty Yangtze. She has been to Chengde, capital of Sichuan, only a few times. She grew up in a neighboring village. But after she married, she came to live in her husband Ligong's home with his brother, his sister-in-law, and their two little girls.

The village where Hungniao lives is a picturesque collection of adobe houses with thatched or tile roofs. Life here moves at a far slower pace than in the big cities to the east. The village has only one dirt lane. A large banyan tree overshadows one end of the lane. On hot summer days, elderly people like to sit on the low wall in its shade and chat.

The lane is fronted on either side by courtyard walls with open gateways. Chickens scratch in the dirt of the courtyards. Pigs grunt in their pens. Along the stream that flows just outside the village, two children in wide-brimmed straw hats herd some ducks lazily paddling in the water.

Hungniao rises at dawn to put on a pot of rice for breakfast and then hurries out to wash clothes in the stream. The equality that is beginning to be practiced between men and women on the coast isn't apparent here. Women still do the cooking and housework, and help in the fields too. They used to have to take care of their small children as well, carrying them to the fields tied to their backs. But

These women are collecting the fertile mud at the bottom of a sluggish stream to spread on their fields.

now the retired women of the village have started a day-care center.

The center is located in a spare room of one of the homes. It doesn't have the modern equipment of city nurseries. But the women who run it are dedicated and loving, and the mothers know they don't need to worry about their children's welfare while they are out in the fields.

Village routines follow the cycle of the year. After the first spring rains, Hungniao and Ligong hitch the iron plow to their buffalo. They drive the buffalo up and down their field, drawing even furrows in the rich red earth.

Seedbeds are sown to rice, and soon in the red plain, patches of sprouting green seedlings shimmer in the sunlight. When rains flood the fields, the work of transplanting begins. One by one, the tiny seedlings taken from the seedbeds must be rerooted in the fields.

Hungniao and Ligong carry the seedlings in aprons tied round their waists. Trousers rolled above their knees, big straw hats bobbing, they move step by step down the field, stooping and rising, stooping and rising, leaving behind neat rows of rice plants poking their slender spikes above the sea of shallow water. Each spike is about a foot from its neighbor. Some nights, tired as she is, Hungniao cannot sleep for the ache in her back.

There's a lull after the planting. The chief need now is water. Drought isn't usual here, but if one should come, irrigation is possible. A large channel branching off from the Min River flows near the village. Ditches leading from the channel carry water to the fields.

As the year progresses, the temperature grows hot and sticky. The villagers return to their homes for a noon meal of rice and vegetables, and a nap afterward. For a while, only the shrilling of the children in the day-care center disturbs the quiet. But presently the older women who are running the center get their charges settled down. Then the hush is broken only by the din of the cicadas in the trees.

By two o'clock, everyone is back at work. There's hoeing and weeding to be done in the vegetable gardens. Silt and weeds must be cleaned out of the channel and the ditches to keep them from clogging. The community-owned pigs and chickens must be tended. Buffaloes must be taken out to graze. And compost has to be gathered. Weeds, manure from pigsties and chicken coops, and human wastes are all carefully collected and dumped in the deep pits dug for this purpose. The noxious conglomeration requires daily stirring until it has aged enough to be used as fertilizer. Then the fertilizer must be ladled out, dipperful by dipperful, on the fields, by people carrying heavy buckets of the stuff swinging from poles balanced on their shoulders.

In the late afternoon, the village comes to life again as people return from the fields. Odors of steaming rice and vegetables fill the air. A breeze moves in the leaves of the big tree at the village entrance. People come out to sit on their doorsteps. And laughing children chase one another up and down the village lane.

Twilight falls. Somewhere a village musician begins to strum his two-stringed fiddle, or erhu. Soon the children are all put to bed. Most of the weary parents quickly join them. But some of the village elders still linger under the old banyan tree, smoking their long pipes and recalling to one another deeds and friends long since gone.

Early summer sees the ripening of the rice, a golden carpet over the red earth. Men and women in broad-brimmed hats go out to their fields with scythes. They reap the rice, gather it in sheaves, thresh it, winnow it, and store it away in baskets. Once this first harvest is in, there's no rest, for the whole cycle must begin again. It is only after the second crop is harvested that the peasants get a short breather, during the fallow time of the year.

Most of the work in the fields has to be done by hand. There are fewer mechanized vehicles here than in the coastal wheat fields. Hungniao and Ligong's hands are cut and scarred by their hard work. There are thick calluses on their palms and the soles of their feet. Their feet are too tough to be hurt now by almost anything they may step on, as they have gone barefoot most of their lives.

Harvesting the rice is done by hand in this paddy.

The Yangs' village is one of several that have been united into a commune. There are many such communes throughout China. The commune provides overall management and services for the villages under it. The headquarters of the Yangs' commune is located in a small town. It contains a few office buildings, a small factory that produces and repairs farm tools, a department store, a hospital, and a high school.

Local affairs are handled by the villages. Each has its own governing committee which has been elected by the villagers themselves. Ligong is a member of his village committee and has been chosen to represent it at the Commune Congresses. These are held periodically in the commune town. At the congresses, government representatives present the yearly production quotas for the commune.

Commune officials discuss the quotas with the representatives of the villages. The quotas are divided among them according to the fertility and amount of land each village tills. The representatives then go home and divide the village quota among the individual families, every one of which is responsible for a particular section of land.

After the harvest is in, the family sells its quota to the government at prices fixed by the state and keeps the proceeds for itself. If the crop surpasses the quota, the family may sell the surplus as it pleases —either to the state or on the open market—and keep these proceeds also. In return, the family pays a low tax to the government and other small amounts to the village and commune. This money goes to building up reserves for such services as schools, health clinics, and hospitals.

This is a new way of doing things in China and is called the Family Responsibility System. It was inaugurated in 1981. Formerly, everyone tilled the land together and received points for the amount of work each did. When the harvests were sold, the proceeds were paid out according to work points. There was little incentive in this way of doing things, and some people didn't even try to meet the quotas.

In addition to the money they get for their grain crops, the peasants have private plots on which they can grow vegetables either for their own use or to sell on the open market. They're also allowed to raise livestock for themselves or for sale. Families in the north keep such domestic animals as sheep and goats. In the south they raise pigs. The Yangs' livestock consists of two pigs and a shoat (a young pig), several chickens and two ducks. The fowl provide the family with eggs.

The government is encouraging the peasants to earn more money by doing handicrafts or making simple utility articles such as cloth shoes, bottles, or bricks in their spare time. The products can be sold on the free market and at county fairs for extra income. This raises the peasants' living standard, which is still below that of city workers.

Hungniao and some of the other women have started a small cooperative that hand-stitches children's embroidered caps and cloth shoes. They have no problem selling these articles at the county fairs that are held from time to time.

The county fair is a festive occasion for the village folk. People gather from all over Sichuan to visit with one another and to purchase homemade products from the stalls.

The fairs are a welcome break in the monotony of country life, where entertainment is scarce. There are no privately owned television sets in the Yangs' village. People are free to watch the one in the community hall if they're not too tired after their long day of work.

Twice a week the village committee meets with the villagers. They take up business matters and discuss politics. Then the talk centers around the part peasants should play in bringing about Modernization of Agriculture, one of the Four Modernizations.

But modernization in the countryside means something quite different from modernization in the city. In the Yangs' little village, there is still no running water. Modernization means being able to draw it from a faucet in the village square instead of having to go down to the irrigation canal to get it. It means electricity on a modest scale—one small light bulb in the kitchen, that is used as little as possible. It means a bicycle, and rubber tires on carts.

To old Shuzhi, it means a toilet that consists of a wooden seat built over the slop jar in his ramshackle outhouse. To the elderly Dengs, it means cooking with methane gas instead of charcoal. The Dengs proudly show their neighbors the covered cesspool behind their house, which is filled with a bubbling putrefying mess. A pipe leading from the cesspool into the kitchen fuels a small gas burner on which Mrs. Deng cooks.

Many things about Hungniao's village are still as primitive as they were at the turn of the century. But the health clinic is something new. It is part of the gigantic health web that the government has woven across the country. There's a clinic or at least one paramedic in almost every village, and a hospital or large health center in most communes. And the county seats have hospitals, although many of them are small, poorly equipped, and understaffed.

A small country hospital.

The clinics and health centers are operated by peasants who have had three to six months of medical training at the commune or county hospital, or by teams of doctors visiting from the big medical colleges in the cities. Because the paramedics are peasants, and peasants work in the fields barefoot, they are called barefoot doctors.

The health clinic staffs give frequent lectures on hygiene to adults and children. They hold periodic campaigns in their villages to get rubbish cleaned up and stagnant pools and ditches filled or sprayed to prevent malaria-bearing mosquitoes from breeding. They launch programs to exterminate rats and flies. And they give inoculations.

All these efforts have paid off. Many diseases, such as cholera, bubonic plague, and smallpox, that were once common in China have almost disappeared. And the life span of the Chinese peasant has been lengthened.

The barefoot doctors aren't allowed to stagnate at their work. Throughout the year they go in rotation to the nearest hospital, to get a two-month brushup course. Most of their training deals with learning new diagnostic skills and how to prepare and use herbal medicines. They are also schooled in acupuncture. Peasants especially have great faith in that treatment, which is centuries old. The equipment consists of a set of slender steel needles that are inserted into various nerve centers of the body to create numbness or stimulate healing.

Herbal medicines are popular too. Chinese doctors have discovered that herbal remedies can be effective in treating a number of simple ailments. The ingredients are easily available to the barefoot doctors, who can gather the herbs from their own locality and prepare them according to hospital formulas.

By late summer, Hungniao no longer goes out to the fields, because she is in her last month of pregnancy, and the midwife at the village health clinic has warned her she must not do any more heavy work until her child is born. All through Hungniao's pregnancy, the midwife, who was trained in her work at the commune hospital, has kept a careful check on the young woman. Prenatal care is an important part of the health clinic's work. It has reduced the number of mother and infant deaths.

Most women have their babies at home. But by periodically checking pregnant women, the midwife can recognize possible complications. Then she will send a woman to the hospital before delivery, to have her baby there.

Now that Hungniao no longer goes to the fields, she is able to help her sister-in-law by taking her youngest niece to the village child-care center. At 8:20 A.M., she sees her older niece off to the village primary school. The cramped one-room school can't compare with city schools. Its walls are bare. The ancient desks and seats are covered with scratches. They are discarded equipment from a Chengde city school, but the villagers are grateful to have them. The teacher who instructs grades one through six is only a junior middle school graduate. Trained teachers are still scarce in China.

In this country schoolhouse, the rooms are bare and the desks are worn. But the children are getting an education—a privilege that used to be reserved for a favored few in China.

Teenagers go to the better equipped junior and senior middle schools at commune headquarters. There the teachers are at least senior middle school graduates. And one has had two years of normal school training at Chengde. But school attendance isn't high in the Yangs' village. Education isn't compulsory, and many parents feel they cannot do without their children's help in the fields. If a family does make a choice between sending a daughter or a son to school, it is the son who is usually elected to go, reflecting the old traditional pattern of favoritism toward males.

Hungniao is hoping her baby will be a boy. It is the dream of every pregnant peasant woman. This is one of the biggest obstacles to bringing birth control to the country. Peasants traditionally not only want large families, but many boys. If the first child is a girl, they will keep on trying.

As the system of rewards and penalties has been having only moderate success in Hungniao's village, the clinic has started to make use of peer pressure. A large chart is posted on the office wall. On the honor list are the names of families who have agreed to limit themselves to one child. In the negative column are the names of those who won't comply. Despite the pressure, however, some women continue to have more than one child.

If Hungniao doesn't get her boy, she may try again.

Gu Ernang of Loessland

In the northwest of China lies a great gray and golden expanse of land—the loess country. It covers the lower slopes of the beetling mountains that hem it in, blankets rolling hills, and forms a vast scarred plateau.

Loess is a German word meaning "windblown silt." The loess-lands are the work of fierce Arctic gales that have been sweeping southward through eons of time. On their way, they pass over the northern deserts, where they scoop up quantities of fine soil, along with silt from dry riverbeds and lakes. The winds carry their loads south, to drop them on a vast expanse that covers almost 205,000 square miles of land and a good part of four provinces. Over all this area, deposits of loess lie from 300 to 1,000 feet deep.

Loess can be found in many other countries, but nowhere else does it cover so large an area as in China. Thousands of gullies scar the land. Some are deep, others shallow. All have been carved by the summer rains. Loess country has only fifteen inches of rain a year. But it often falls in torrents when it comes.

Then freshets start streaming down rolling hills and across the plateau lands, carving new gullies in the soft silt and deepening old ones. Eventually the water, laden with silt, enters the Yellow River, China's second largest waterway. It is the soil of loess country that the river has been carrying eastward to build up the North China Plain.

Eighteen-year-old Gu Ernang lives in one of the poorest sections of loessland. His straggling dusty village is made up of an assortment of dwelling places. Some are small earthen houses. To build them, parallel board frames are set up about a foot and a half apart. The space between the frames is filled with layers of loess, which is tamped down with heavy posts to compact the mass and give it strength. When the frames are taken away, the solid wall between them remains.

Other homes are caves dug in the cliff walls. Ernang lives in one of these. For centuries, the people of loessland have been digging cave homes in cliffs and hillsides. It is easy work, because the soil is so soft. But once exposed to air, the inner surfaces harden so that there is little chance of a collapse.

The cave homes have many advantages. They are economical to make and much more comfortable than regular houses in this region of extreme hot and cold temperatures. In summer they remain cool, in winter warm. This is very important in a country where fuel is scarce.

But the cave homes can be dangerous also, for the loesslands are in earthquake country. One of the worst earthquakes of the century took place here in the twenties. Then homes and storage places, along with hundreds of people and animals, were buried in the shifting silt. Ernang's grandfather still speaks in awe of "the day the mountains walked."

In more prosperous areas of loessland, the cave houses are neatly faced with brick or cement. They have wide entranceways with attractive latticework and well-turned doors. Their windows are covered with glass or opaque paper. Some contain several rooms. The chimney is a tunnel that leads through the loess to an outside vent. It carries off the smoke of the kitchen stove.

But Ernang's home is just a couple of crude rooms dug into a cliff. There are no windows. The front door is a tattered matting that hangs askew. Ernang lives here with his parents, grandparents, and younger brother. His older sister has married and moved away.

Ernang's skin is rough and gritty from the soft penetrating silt that has worked into his pores. His throat seems always dry, his nostrils caked. He goes barefoot, and his faded gray clothes have been patched many times. They are full of silt too. It's hard to keep clean in this land where water is so scarce most of the year.

In the winter, loess country lies naked and harsh under the bitter winds that blow down from the north, filling the sky with a dull haze. When the winds rise to gale force, the dust becomes a yellow fog that darkens the sky and burns the throat and eyes and nostrils, driving indoors all those who have no pressing work to do.

In late spring, after the first rainfall, hills and plateaus alike put on a shimmering green mantle of young wheat or millet. By summer, loess country has become a lush, waving sea. This is the critical period. If no rains fall, the rich green of the fields quickly yellows, then turns into a sea of parched brown stalks rustling mournfully in every gust of wind.

If the rains come in torrents, flash floods rush down the steep terraced hills, washing away the maturing fields of grain and filling the cultivated valleys below with rubble. Over the centuries, drought and flood have resulted in widespread famines in which millions have died.

Improved transportation now enables the government to send supplies to the stricken areas. The immense problem of erosion remains, however, and scientists are working with peasants in an effort to solve it. Earthworks have been thrown up across small ravines to hold the floods back from surrounding fields. The water that the small catchment basins collect can also serve for irrigation in dry seasons. More than 8,000 larger reservoirs have also been built. But catchment basins and reservoirs silt up rapidly, making them useless within three to ten years.

However, the soil of loessland is fertile. And if all goes well, by autumn Ernang goes out into a rich world carpeted with golden grain. The countryside becomes alive with energetic human beings, scything the wheat, then threshing and stacking it, and finally loading it onto carts harnessed to donkeys that haul it off to the villages.

Ernang does his share. He has been working in the fields since he was old enough to glean the harvested wheat or carry a hoe. He has had only two years of schooling. But it is no less than the other

Harvest time in loessland, on the outskirts of Lanzhou.

children of his village. When they're too young to work, they attend classes in a small cave with a junior-middle-school graduate for their teacher. Desks and chairs are made out of compacted loess. Books and pencils are few and have to be shared. As the children grow older, they spend less and less time at school. During much of the year, they are too useful in the fields to be spared.

Ernang's cramped home is the scene of frequent family quarrels. Though the government is trying to provide more housing in the country as well as in the city, it is almost impossible to do so in poor areas like Ernang's. Ernang's grandparents cause most of the trouble. Elderly people in the hinterlands are much more conservative than those along the eastern seaboard. Ernang's grandparents expect blind obedience from their children and grandchildren.

The current argument is over Ernang. When Ernang was sixteen, he joined the militia, which is made up of volunteers. There are militia units throughout the country, composed of peasants, factory workers, miners, and government officials. The recruits go through military training and learn first aid. They form a vast volunteer force that stands ready to help the army in case of natural disaster or enemy attack.

Ernang has enjoyed being a member of the militia. Several times a week he trudges two miles through the dusty land to the little commune headquarters town where a People's Liberation Army post is located. Here he and other recruits from the commune do military drills, practice target shooting and throwing hand grenades, and learn some first aid skills. Ernang has found this a welcome relief from the monotonous grind of farm work. He likes the lectures the post lieutenant gives after the training sessions.

In glowing terms, the lieutenant describes the soldiers' traditional devotion to the people. Soldiers of the People's Liberation Army help in the fields when needed. They build roads and dams and do other construction work to improve conditions. They are always on call when disaster strikes.

The lieutenant gives his young recruits a brief history lesson on the origins of the People's Liberation Army. Back in 1921, he tells them, the Communist Party was founded in Shanghai. In four years it grew rapidly, attracting poor peasants and underpaid city workers.

Meanwhile Dr. Sun Yat-sen, whose revolutionary army had overthrown the Manchu dynasty, had set up his Nationalist government, known as the Kuomintang, in Canton. But the Kuomintang was not strong enough to take over China, which was ruled by numbers of warlords. In 1925, shortly before Dr. Sun Yat-sen died, the Communists and the Kuomintang joined forces to drive out the warlords. The Communists, under Mao Zedong, were to enlist the aid of the peasants and workers, and incite them to sabotage and work stoppages. The Kuomintang Army, under Chiang Kai-shek, the Kuomintang generalissimo, was to do the actual fighting.

The Northern Campaign, as it was called, was successful. But as Chiang Kai-shek reached Shanghai and saw victory in his grasp, he turned on his Communist allies and began a wholesale massacre. This launched a wide scale civil war. Only a few Communists, including Mao Zedong, managed to escape Chiang Kai-shek's purge. They made their way to the Chingkang-shan range in Hunan province, where as time went by they were joined by others. It was in these mountains that the famous Red Army was formed.

In 1933, Chiang Kai-shek's superior numbers managed to drive the small Red Army out of its stronghold in Hunan. The Communist forces, which now consisted of some 100,000 soldiers, began beating a retreat toward another Communist stronghold whose headquarters were at Yenan, deep in loessland, far to the northwest. Many of the soldiers were accompanied by their wives and children, swelling their number to 200,000.

It was a long, terrible journey. All the way, the Red Army was harassed by Kuomintang forces. It had to scale high snow-clad mountains and travel through dangerous Tibetan bogs. The cruel journey lasted 386 days. Only some 7,000 of those who had set out upon it reached Yenan. The historic trek came to be known as the Long March.

In Yenan, the Red Army continued to grow. It played an important part in the struggle against Japan, which in 1937 had invaded China and taken Beijing, Shanghai, and Nanjing (Nanking). These events occurred at the beginning of World War II. When the war came to an end with the defeat of Japan, the Red Army and the Kuomintang forces began a fierce struggle again. Finally the Kuomintang armies were driven off the China mainland and onto the island of Taiwan. On October 1, 1949, Mao Zedong declared the founding of the People's Republic of China. The Red Army's name was changed to the People's Liberation Army and became the military branch of the new government.

The lieutenant's fervor, as he recounts all this, imparts a dream to Ernang. He decides he wants to join the army. Now that he has turned eighteen, he is eligible for the draft. China's Military Service Law requires all young men who come of age to register for the army. They are given a physical checkup and then screened to see if they are good army material. If they are passed by their local recruiting office, they are inducted.

Ernang's usefulness in the fields and his activities in the militia would probably exempt him from army service. But Ernang wants to join, and his parents are satisfied with his choice. They see it as an opportunity for Ernang to improve his life.

The army post lieutenant has been impressed by Ernang's enthusiasm and the skill he has shown in his militia training. He would like to have the young man in the army. But Ernang's grandparents are throwing up obstacles. Why should Ernang he taken away from the family when he is already doing his share as a militia member, they want to know. In the army he will get only a very small allowance at first—not enough to send any money home. And his family needs his help in the fields.

Ernang has to listen to this scolding day and night. He becomes sulky, then belligerent. Sometimes he even refuses to go to the fields to work. His parents are so tired of the stream of constant complaints that they threaten to throw the old couple out of the cave home.

But everyone knows they won't really do this. It would get them into trouble with the law which states that children, if possible, must provide for elderly parents who have no other means of support.

The village committee tries to smooth out the quarrels, but Ernang's grandparents order them from the cave when they take his side. Finally the army lieutenant comes personally to talk things over with the old people. He points out that it is Ernang's duty to serve his country, and their duty to support him in this decision. Using the same eloquence that won Ernang, he reminds them of the old days when they suffered under greedy landlords and how they were liberated by the dedicated Red Army. Surely their gratitude will cause them to relinquish their grandson to serve in the army now and so repay a past debt.

With the matter put this way, the old couple can no longer object without losing face. They nod their heads glumly, and the lieutenant continues: "True, in the beginning your grandson will get a mere allowance," he points out. "But he will soon be drawing a salary. And you, as the family of a serviceman, will receive many benefits from the government. If he should be killed in action or die in the line of duty, he will be given the honorable title of martyr. And his family will get a pension from the government."

In the end, Ernang receives his grandparents' grudging blessing and is inducted into the army. He is sent to a barracks just outside the city of Lanzhou, an industrial and agricultural center that stands on the banks of the Yellow River in a fertile basin surrounded by loess country. He is issued an army uniform and boots, and a green cap with a red star in front. His military training continues, and he also attends night classes to further his education.

Ernang spends some of his time helping to till the army fields and care for its hogs. Most of the soldiers' food supplies come from their own farm. Barracks across the country are surrounded by similar farms which are tilled by the soldiers stationed there. This tradition started during the revolutionary years, to keep the army from being a burden on the peasants and thus winning their goodwill.

The soldiers wash and mend their own clothes, as well as cook their own meals. They have their own hospital and medical staff. In times of emergency, these facilities are used to help civilians.

Only a few women have been inducted into the army. Most of them do specialized jobs. Some are nurses in the hospitals. Others take care of nurseries for the children of army men. Several women have joined the air force as pilots.

Ernang finds life in the barracks much easier than on the dusty farm he has left. His horizons are rapidly widening. He is the first one in his family to visit Lanzhou. Ernang's first sight of the city, where some two million people live, fills him with wonder.

He gapes at the great modern bridge that crosses the Yellow River. Buildings sprawl along both banks. He gets a crick in his neck looking at the lofty smokestacks of oil refineries and petrochemical plants that are spilling their pollution into the air. The blue skies here are dulled with a noxious gray haze caused by the furnaces that provide electric power by burning coal from nearby mines.

Recently, however, the new Liuqia (Liuchia) dam built upstream on the Yellow River has been contributing hydroelectric power as well. One holiday, Ernang and some of his fellow recruits take a bus for a sight-seeing trip to the dam. Standing on the small lake wharf, they are astonished to find that the turgid yellow river that flows through Lanzhou becomes a broad expanse of clear water above the dam. And they cannot turn their eyes from the tall metal framework of the hydroelectric station, silhouetted against the sky.

Ernang and his friends hire the boatman of a small motor ferry to take them on a ride over the man-made lake. Ernang looks down at the motorboat as his companions clamber into it. He has never seen so much water before. He hangs back fearfully until his companions force him into the boat.

Ernang sits down quickly and clings to the side of the small ferry. The boat moves up the quiet lake, framed in craggy mountain buttresses, and Ernang gradually relaxes. The waters seem to stretch away forever, until the boat enters a winding inlet and the barren cliffs draw closer. They revolve before Ernang's eyes, great saw-toothed jumbles of cliff and rock. Finally, after more than an hour, they fall away and Ernang finds himself looking at a spit of beach. It fronts a narrow valley surrounded by steep wild hills. To the left rises a high sandstone cliff. In its center, a great statue of Buddha, carved out of the soft sandstone, looks down on the valley. On either side, the cliff is pocked with rows of cave shrines, some small, others larger, arranged in tiers. Ernang and his comrades have been plunged back into history, for this is ancient Bingling, or One Hundred Thousand Buddhas Monastery, now a national museum.

The motorboat draws up to the beach. Splashing a little in the shallow water, Ernang and his companions scramble ashore. They cross the soggy meadow to the cliff. A scaffolding that fronts its face supports flights of wooden steps up which tourists are clambering. Ernang and his friends mount tier after tier to enter the shrines one by one. Each is inhabited by carved images of Buddha and his followers. In some, the ceilings and the images are sooty from generations of incense.

These are all just curiosities to Ernang and his companions. They know little about Buddhism or that it was founded in India by a young prince who left home to seek enlightenment. He was called the Gautama Buddha, and the Buddhist religion which is founded on his teachings quickly spread throughout India. From India it entered China. Early Chinese Buddhist monks founded the Bingling monastery. Generation after generation of monks carved out these shrines and images for rich donors who hoped to earn merit in a future life by honoring Buddha in this way. The images reveal how over the centuries Buddhism was transformed from a foreign to a native religion.

As the afternoon grows late, the young men scramble down the scaffolding steps to the valley below. Ernang stops to look back at the great orange face of the cliff pocked with its many caves. In the center, the huge brooding Buddha seems to gaze down upon him with a severe rebuke. Suddenly he feels small and lonely.

The great carved Buddha, central figure of the Bingling monastery on the Yellow River, looks out sternly from a sandstone cliff that is pocked with small cave shrines.

A stupa, or prayer tower, marks the grave of a Buddhist monk in a monastery.

Then a child's voice behind him cries admiringly, "Look, mother. Soldiers! Soldiers!"

"Very brave, our soldiers!" his mother answers proudly.

Ernang straightens his cap with the red star on it, pulls down his tunic, throws back his shoulders. He turns away from the brooding Buddha and walks jauntily toward the beach where the launch is waiting.

The Ancient Valley

Some young people in China are following professions that take them to out-of-the-way places. Teams of college students led by experienced geologists are making large-scale surveys of little-known regions in search of hidden mineral resources. Most young people in China today are not too interested in their ancient literature and art. But some are enthusiastically entering the fields of paleontology and archaeology and are working in widely scattered digs to discover more of their country's past.

The Chinese Society of Archaeologists now numbers about 600 members, and thirteen universities in China provide undergraduate majors in the subject while one offers a doctorate. Twenty-one-year old Hu Jiangsu is one of the young archaeologists. She lives in far western Xian (Sian), which stands in a wide valley watered by the Wei River, an important tributary of the Yellow River. The whole Wei Valley is a treasure house of China's ancient history and past glories. The capitals of three of the country's most important dynasties were located in the fine natural fortification afforded by the surrounding mountains.

The first man to unite China into a single empire was Qin (Chin) Shi Huang Di, which means First Emperor of the Qin. His capital lay about nine miles northwest of Xian.

The Qin were followed by the Han, who called their capital Changan. It stood on the banks of the Wei, four and a half miles to the northeast of present-day Xian. The Han ruled from 206 B.C. to A.D. 220. During their long reign, they increased the size of the empire and sent their armies through the deserts of Xinjiang to establish trade with the West. They became so powerful that their influence was felt around the world. The Chinese of that day began calling themselves the Sons of Han. The term "Han Chinese" is still used today to distinguish the majority people from the minority nationalities that live in China.

The last great dynasty to have its capital in the valley of the Wei was the Tang, which ruled from A.D. 618 to 907. Its capital, which was also called Changan, stood on the very site of present-day Xian.

When Jiangsu was thirteen, her uncle took her to see the ruins that still mark Changan's old West Market Place. He pointed out the deep wheel ruts that trace the ancient thoroughfare.

"They were made by the wheels of chariots and carriages in which elegant young noblemen and royal ladies, screened from public gaze, went on shopping sprees," he told Jiangsu. "And these were the shops where they spent their money."

He pointed out the ruins of thousands of shops that lined the roadway.

"When Changan finally fell to rebel forces, the merchants fled without taking time to remove all their goods. So archaeologists have been able to find out what kind of merchandise was sold in the different shops."

As they walked along the ruins, Jiangsu's uncle pointed out shops for her. "This one contained remnants of silk. It was owned by Chinese merchants. In this one, some ancient wine casks were found. It probably belonged to Persians. And in one of these shops, archaeologists discovered ornaments set with pearls and agates, some made of crystal, others of gold. Their designs and workmanship showed they came from the West. So these shops must have belonged to Arab traders. There were a lot of Persian and Arab traders in old Changan, you know."

Jiangsu showed so much interest in antiquities that her uncle invited her to go with him to visit an archaeologist friend who was working at the first emperor's palace complex. Excavation had begun there in 1974. Jiangsu was amazed at how archaeologists are able to reconstruct a whole palace out of some ancient ruins.

"Here is the gallery," her uncle's friend, who was showing them around, explained. "The rooms that open on it probably belonged to the ladies-in-waiting. See the earthen beds against the wall? This room with the huge earthenware drain was probably a bathroom."

As they mounted to the second tier, the archaeologist pointed out a great expanse of vermilion floor over which rose the ruins of two-story-high walls, still bright with bold murals.

"This was probably the first emperor's banquet room," he told his guests.

On the third tier they came out on a terrace overlooking the vast Wei Valley, dreaming in the sunlight. Standing there, Jiangsu felt a sudden chill. Here, more than two thousand years ago, a thirteen-year-old emperor, no older than herself, had sworn that his empire would last for ten times ten thousand years. But he had died at the age of forty-nine, after only thirty-six years of rule, and his dynasty died with him.

The palace ruins are not the only memento of Qin Shi Huang Di's reign. His 2,200-year-old burial mound stands about thirty miles east of Xian. It still awaits excavation by archaeologists, who do not want to open it until they have developed modern means of preservation to protect its priceless contents. They are afraid that otherwise the ancient treasures in the tomb may disintegrate when exposed to the air.

But in 1974–75, an exciting discovery was made in the nearby plain. That year a serious drought struck the region around Xian. Peasants on the outskirts of the city began sinking wells in search of water. In their digging, they came upon some broken pottery figures of men and horses.

The government has asked everyone throughout the country to be on the alert for such artifacts and to report them at once. Unfortunately, in many localities, in their zeal to implement the Four Modernizations, people have been carelessly bulldozing priceless relics as they break new ground for factories or fields. Other losses are caused by some daring grave robbers. Despite the risk of heavy penalties if discovered, they manage to dig up ancient tombs, steal the contents, and sell them to foreign dealers.

Fortunately, when the peasants in the Wei Valley discovered the pottery shards, they stopped work at once and notified the Xian authorities. Trained research teams soon arrived on the scene and began excavations. The vaults they found held life-size pottery warriors and horses, some whole, most shattered. They had been placed there to serve the first emperor in his afterlife. Archaeologists estimate that when the pottery warriors and horses are restored, they will number some 7,000.

As the archaeologists' work progressed, the government built a huge building like an airplane hangar over the area to protect the pottery figures and to give some shelter to the staff working there. The hangar was turned into a museum where, for a few fen, visitors are admitted. Crosswalks above the trenches allow visitors to walk through the great hangar, looking at the completed figures or watching the archaeology apprentices working among the broken pottery shards.

During the years she was in senior middle school, Jiangsu visited the hangar museum often. Each time she went, she saw new pottery figures filling up the trenches. Some stood, others knelt. All were strong-faced men, some with drooping mustaches. Most were dressed in battle tunics, leggings, and sandals, with long hair done up in topknots. A few, obviously generals, wore breastplates, caps with tails, and boots on their feet. Among them stood life-size

The hangarlike building houses Qin Shi Huang Di's pottery warriors outside the city of Xian. Inside, young archaeologists work out the puzzles of broken shards, which when properly numbered and glued together will form a warrior or a horse.

pottery horses in groups of four. But the weapons the warriors once held, and the wooden and leather chariots to which the horses were harnessed, had vanished. They had either rotted away or were destroyed by a great fire set by vandals who swept through the vaults centuries ago, looting, and shattering the pottery soldiers and horses.

Upon graduation from senior middle school, Jiangsu took the college entrance examinations and passed them. She was accepted by a Xian university where she specialized in archaeology. This spring she graduated and began working full time at the hangar site.

Because of the muggy summer heat, almost everyone in Xian begins the workday at 7:30 A.M. So Jiangsu must rise early if she wants to get in some calisthenics before she catches the bus that carries her to the digs. Since all China runs on the same time as Beijing, the sun rises much later in the west. And Jiangsu has to do her exercises in the dark. She goes to a little square near her home to join other early risers who are led through their drills by a coach.

Exercise period over, she has a quick breakfast of noodles and vegetables and then hurries to board her bus. It rattles down a highway that cuts through the broad plain. On either side stretch fields of wheat and corn and sesame, interspersed with gardens of cabbages, peppers, onions, and yard-long string beans hanging from frames.

Here and there, fields of golden sunflowers turn their faces eastward to catch the morning sun. Their ripened seeds will be gathered. Some will be dried and salted for snacks. Most will be pressed into oil. Now that the corn is ripe, Jiangsu sees children in the little adobe villages along the way, munching on corn on the cob.

Once at the digs, Jiangsu enters one of the trenches, crouches down beside a heap of broken pottery pieces, and begins her work. Carefully she sorts out the shards, examines each closely, and then numbers it. Later a skilled artisan will piece the shards together by number to make a whole figure.

At 11:30, everyone breaks for a siesta that lasts until 2:30 P.M. Jiangsu has time to go home, have a bowl of noodles and vegetables, and take a nap. She returns to the digs at 2:30 and works until 6:30. The sun is still high in the sky when she starts for home, because sunset comes much later here than on the east coast.

Xian is a quiet city. Young people who come to it to work from places like Beijing and Shanghai complain there's nothing to do. But Jiangsu, who has spent all her life in Xian, is satisfied. Sometimes she and her friends attend one of the open-air theaters, to watch a live show or see a movie. Sometimes they visit an amusement park where they can get up a basketball or volleyball game or just stroll around.

Sunday is a big day for everyone. Then farmers come in from the

Above, *a great deal of family living and playing goes on in the narrow side streets that branch off Xian's main thoroughfares.* Below, *wistful children sit dreaming by a lake at Huaching Hot Springs outside Xian.*

countryside to sight-see. And city people enjoy relaxing in front of their doors. Many of the little girls are dressed in holiday clothes— long pink silk skirts and blouses or jackets with tinsel trimmings. Big bows, usually pink or gray, are perched on their heads. The Chinese call such bows butterfly knots.

The boys are less formally dressed. Most of them are in T-shirts and shorts that reach just below the knee. Small children with the seats cut out of their pants or with no pants at all run around squealing. Babies and small children in China dress like that until they are toilet trained.

Sunday is also a day for Jiangsu to attend to household chores. Her eight-year-old sister, Chenrong, does her part by vigorously scrubbing the towels in a big washtub at the front door, drawing her water from the neighborhood faucet.

These city girls are busy doing their Sunday wash. Shoes as well as clothes are scrupulously washed.

When Jiangsu finishes her work, she puts on her best clothes and jumps on her bicycle.

"Where are you going, Jiangsu?" her sister calls after her.

Jiangsu doesn't answer. Neighborhood women preparing the noon meal on small braziers outside their doors turn to watch her.

"Going to meet a boyfriend?" one of them asks.

Jiangsu blushes and pedals on at a brisk pace. The odors of cooking follow her. Under an awning, some workmen are already enjoying a meal of noodles and vegetables. Farther on, Jiangsu passes a group of men playing a spirited game of cards. From somewhere nearby she hears snatches of an old folk song.

Jiangsu pedals down lane after lane, finally coming into a wide thoroughfare. She follows it out of the city into a countryside that is almost deserted of people today. The hot sun pours down on her but she doesn't slow her pace. A bicyclist like herself appears on the road ahead. He looks over his shoulder and stops, allowing Jiangsu to catch up with him. It is Mi Holan, one of the young archaeologists.

"You're here at last, Jiangsu," he says, laughing.

Jiangsu nods. They pedal along together in silence. Jiangsu and Mi Holan have been going together for a whole year. But they have to meet secretly because they know their families would never approve. Holan is a Hui, while Jiangsu is a Han. The Huis are descendants of the early Arab traders who came to Changan during Tang days. The Tang emperors welcomed them and invited them to stay if they chose. Many did so, bringing their religion with them. They built mosques, where their religious leaders, imams, read the Koran and conducted services.

The Arabs adopted small Chinese girls, brought them up in the Moslem faith, and then married them. The children of these families then married among themselves, keeping their Moslem religion and customs. They came to be known as Hui.

For centuries the Hui have been living in this part of China. They look like Chinese because the Arab strain has become very diluted.

Only here and there can people be seen who have rounder eyes and sharper noses with higher bridges. And there are a few with curly hair.

In Xian the Hui live in their own neighborhoods which surround two old mosques. Usually only older people attend the services there. But though most modern Hui do not follow their religion, they still keep some of their strict religious laws. Most of them will not eat pork. Even their cattle, sheep, and fowl must be slaughtered in the proper Moslem way, so they have their own butchers, food shops, and restaurants.

After the days of the Tang, animosity sprang up between the Han and the Hui. Young Hans liked to torment the Hui by fastening bits of pork or pictures of pigs on their butcher shops and even their mosques. In some places the goaded Hui rose in revolt. There were bloody massacres in which whole cities were left in ruins.

The hatred between the two peoples continued into modern times. But when the soldiers of the Red Army came to Hui regions, their commanders gave them strict orders to respect the Moslem

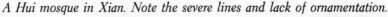

A Hui mosque in Xian. Note the severe lines and lack of ornamentation.

A Hui family living in the Moslem section of Xian. Though mother and son look Han, the grandfather's nose with its high bridge gives him away as a Hui.

people and their religion. The Hui in turn came to trust the Red Army. A battalion of Hui even joined the Communist forces in their struggle against the Japanese. Later they fought against the Kuomintang in the Civil War.

Since the founding of the People's Republic of China, the government has been working to improve relations between the Han and the Hui. Though these efforts were suspended during the Cultural Revolution, they have been renewed in the years following 1976. But mutual distrust remains between the two peoples. And this feeling is far stronger in the hinterlands than in the coastal cities where seafaring Arabs also settled. Even though they may be on friendly terms, Hans and Huis do not want their children to marry each other.

Jiangsu and Holan are caught between the two conflicting cultures. They are in love and want to marry. But they are afraid of their parents' anger. They don't want to be ostracized, so they don't even let their friends know that they are meeting. They choose these outings in the countryside where the risk of being seen together is not so great. Today their destination is the site of the large Neolithic village of Banpo. It lies about six miles out of Xian, overlooking the Chan River. Carbon dating shows the village to be about 8,000 years old.

From a wooden walkway, Jiangsu and Holan look out over the quiet site where here and there a few reconstructed replicas stand on the foundations of old dwelling places. They are small windowless mud huts with the doors all opening to the south, their backs turned to the north from which the cold winter winds blow.

It is apparent from tools and bones found on the site that the villagers knew how to farm and that they kept domestic animals such as sheep and dogs. Their tools were stone axes and spades and wooden hoes. They sewed their clothes with bone needles. Their arrowheads were made of stone or bone.

The remains of crude kilns show that they had learned how to fire their pottery, which is decorated with colorful designs. They must have been a happy people to make such playful pictures, Jiangsu thinks, and she remembers that they are her ancestors.

Banpo was a matriarchal village. Women provided what little government there was. They, rather than the men, passed on their names to their children. When the graves in the village cemetery were opened, they all revealed the same number and kind of artifacts in each. This meant there were no rich or poor in those days. It was only later that tribes developed, male chiefs arose, and wars began. Legend describes those ancient times as a golden period of peace and harmony. Jiangsu turns and catches Holan's hand in hers.

"How simple things must have been," she whispers. "There were no Han or Hui then."

"Just people," Holan answers. "Just people like you and me."

The Sea of Death

Pelud and Kunvad Timur live in China's far west Xinjiang region. They belong to the Uygur nationality.

There are fifty-seven different nationalities in China. The one with the largest number is called the Han. The Han Chinese are the majority people. Because there are far fewer members of the other nationalities, they are known as the minority peoples. Wherever large numbers of a minority people are gathered in one place, the government has given them full control of local matters, with government representatives acting as advisers.

The large areas that have local control are called Autonomous Regions, the smaller ones Autonomous Districts. There are five Autonomous Regions. The Xinjiang Uygur Autonomous Region is one of them. It lies in China's far west, sharing borders with the Central Asian republics of the Soviet Union. Though several different minority nationalities live in Xinjiang, the greatest number are Uygurs.

A Uygur mother and her daughter.

Pelud and Kunvad are Uygurs. They have their own language—
a musical tongue that is quite different from Han Chinese. And
though their hair and eyes are dark, they don't look like the Han.
Their eyes are rounder and their noses have higher bridges. Kunvad's
long hair is brown rather than black and has a curl to it.

Kunvad always wears a scarf over her head when she goes outside.
The Timurs, like most Uygurs, are Moslems, and the scarf takes the
place of the veil used by Moslem women in the Arab countries. The
men wear jackets and trousers like the Han, but the women's clothes
are different—loose dresses worn over long loose pants.

The Timurs' home village is a tiny cluster of flat-roofed adobe
houses. It stands in a green oasis on the south side of the towering
Tianshan Range, which divides Xinjiang in half and forms the northern boundary of the Tarim Basin. The basin is almost completely

Two Uygur children stand in a gateway leading down to an oasis village. The house below has a flat roof, as sloping roofs are not necessary in this land of scant rainfall.

enclosed by mountains. The Pamirs rise in the far west. The massive Kunluns hem in the south.

Lying in the heart of Asia, blocked on three sides by mountains, the Tarim Basin is very hot and dry, averaging less than four inches of rain a year. The center of the basin is taken up by the great Taklamakan Desert, which covers some 11,532 square miles and is one of the largest and driest deserts in the world. Cultivation can take place only on the oases that fringe the bases of the Tianshan and Kunlun ranges. Here streams, swollen by melting snows, flow down to build up broad alluvial fans.

Farther on, the streams are either evaporated by the scorching desert sun or they sink underground. For centuries the Uygurs have been reclaiming the desert lands by digging tunnels and lining them with stones. They channel the water through these tunnels. Open culverts at intervals enable the farmers to pump what they need into irrigation ditches. Knowledge of how to build such tunnels, which are called karez, was brought long ago from ancient Persia.

The Timurs' village stands on land that has just recently been reclaimed. It is surrounded on three sides by rippling waves of sand and great tawny dunes. In the midst of the golden wastes, the little oasis gleams like an emerald, a refreshing sight of green wheat and cornfields, of pleasant vegetable gardens, small vineyards, and fruit orchards. Shade trees grow in rows, forming shelter belts around fields, orchards, and village houses.

The little oasis seems to be flourishing, but there are problems. Though the surface of the land is arid, the underground water table is high, swollen by all the streams that have sunk into it. Irrigation raises the level even higher. If it reaches the saturation point, dense reeds spring up in the fields, choking out the wheat. The underground water may also be so brackish that as it rises, it kills the crops. The villagers have had to build stone-lined drainage ditches to carry off used water.

But the greatest threat is always the desert. The Uygurs call it the sea of death. Under the winds, the sands are almost as fluid as the

Mother, daughter, and grandfather stand under the poplars of their oasis village. A head covering of some sort in place of a veil is usually worn by Uygur women when out of doors. Men wear a cornered cap.

waves of the sea. To hold them back from fields and village, the Uygurs have planted row after row of shelter trees. They have also crisscrossed the nearest dunes with gridirons of tough desert grass and low bushes, in hopes that the gridirons will keep the dunes anchored in place. The Uygurs call them sand nets.

It takes the cooperation of everyone in the village to fight this battle against the mighty desert. But most of the people who live here are related in some way, and the reclamation of the land is a family affair.

Pelud and Kunvad live with Pelud's parents in one of the thick-walled adobe houses. Their kitchen stove is made of adobe also. Kunvad and her mother-in-law bake the Uygurs' favorite bread in its big oven. The bread, which is called shinang, is made of unleavened flour mixed with water. The women shape the dough into flat disks that they slap against the sides of the oven. They bake the bread until it becomes so hard it sometimes has to be softened by dunking it in tea before it can be eaten.

The Timurs' beds are adobe platforms over which colorful blankets are spread. The largest is in the living room. It is the bed of the older Timurs, who also say their prayers on it.

Most of the time the family members take their meals outside in the arbor, under the trellis of grapevines. Here a cloth runner is spread over a coarse floor rug, and the dishes are set out on it—steamed buns, noodles with bits of mutton or chicken, vegetables, shinang, and whatever fruit is in season. It is all washed down with brick tea, which is made of both leaves and stems pressed tightly together. Chunks of the brick are broken off and boiled to brew the strong bitter tea.

The younger Timurs are only twenty-three years old, but they already have three small children. The oldest is four and the youngest is six months. The couple were in their teens when, with the blessing of their families, they went through the Uygur wedding rites. No age limit for marriage is set for minority nationalities. And they are not asked to practice birth control since most of the regions where they live are underpopulated.

The Timurs rise very early to do their hard work during the cool dawn hours. They weed and fertilize, clean out irrigation ditches and karez. During the plowing, sowing, and harvesting seasons, father Timur helps the young couple. The rest of the year he takes care of

Melons, especially the sweet Hami melon grown nowhere else in the world, are specialties of these Uygur vendors along the roadside outside the city of Urumchi.

the livestock. Since all the villagers are Moslems, none of them has pigs. Instead the Timur family owns two donkeys, some chickens, and a few sheep. The old man takes the sheep to graze and, with the help of his wife, delivers the lambs when the ewes are birthing. Once a year he does the shearing.

Old Mrs. Timur cooks and cleans house and cares for the children. She also spends a lot of time spinning the fleece of the sheep into yarn that she weaves into rugs and bed coverings on a hand loom. Kunvad joins her mother-in-law at this work whenever she has time. The colorful rugs that lie on the floor or are folded up at the foot of the beds and the gay woven tapestries that hang on the walls have all been made by the two women.

As the day progresses, the desert heat rapidly mounts. It reaches its peak around two o'clock in the afternoon. Then the surface temperature of the sand may climb as high as 200 degrees Fahrenheit. Cool air meeting hot air produces whirlwinds that go spinning through the village like golden dervishes, stinging the eyes and face with grit.

During the heat of the day, the Timurs and the other villagers take a lengthy siesta. Then as the westering sun sends giant shadows across the dunes, they finish the day's chores. With the setting sun, the temperature drops quickly. In the winter it may fall below zero, but in the summertime it's pleasantly cool. The Timurs enjoy sitting in their arbor after the evening meal.

Father Timur entertains his family. Strumming on his dutar, a two-stringed Uygur fiddle, he sings the folk songs of his people. Sometimes he tells stories about the ancient silk roads. There were two of these roads. One skirted the foot of the Tianshan Range. The other ran along the foot of the Kunluns to the south. Altogether it took a year or more for the caravans that passed along these routes to reach Changan from their homes in the far west.

The Timurs' village stands near the northern silk road. And as father Timur talks, Kunvad seems to see again the long procession of camels, bells tinkling at their necks. They stop here at the oasis, to water their animals and purchase provisions before going on. The traders and merchants that accompany the caravans are a motley lot, traveling together only because there's safety in numbers. There are Arabs in long white robes, and Greeks, Romans, Parsees, and Persians in woolen tunics and pantaloons, in long cloaks and leather boots and pointed hats. The babble of their voices speaking different tongues fills the air.

Father Timur says that once fierce nomads roamed the upper slopes of the Tianshan Range. From there they would swoop down to raid the desert kingdoms and the caravans. Han emperors set up garrisons along the way to guard the silk routes.

But the Han forces could not protect the travelers from the dangers of the Taklamakan itself. Some of the travelers would succumb to desert heat. Others, frozen by winter gales, would die of pneumonia. Fierce windstorms would rise to buffet and blind them all with curtains of thick yellow sand. During these times, travelers became separated from the main body of the caravan.

"There was no hope for them then," father Timur sighs. "For the voices of the dead would call out to them. And they would hear the sound of feet marching, marching, to the piping of the fifes. They would hurry toward the voices, to join the ghostly army, and wander farther and farther away to their death."

Father Timur sighs again.

"I myself have heard those voices too," he whispers. "Right here in the desert near our own village. But I know better than to follow them out there."

He waves a hand at the sand dunes, ghostly in the starlight.

Kunvad and Pelud nod their heads, for they have heard the voices also. Scientists may explain that the sounds are caused by electrically charged grains of mineral sands grating against one another as they slide down the dunes. But to the Timurs, who live on the fringe of the desert, the ghosts are very real.

Sometimes when the winds howl over the tiny village at night, the Timur children wake up terrified and sobbing. Then Kunvad, who is as frightened as they, comforts them as best she can. She and Pelud know that more than the bones of solitary travelers lie out there. As winds blow away whole companies of sand dunes, the ruins of once flourishing cities, buried for centuries, suddenly come to light again. In these melancholy places, there are doors hanging ajar in crumbled walls, houses with collapsed roofs, and whitened skeletons staring at the sky. The ground is strewn with ancient Chinese and Greek and Roman coins, pots, bronze jugs, and remnants of silk gowns.

After the wind tempests have blown themselves out, Pelud and Kunvad often find that despite the nets of sand and the belts of shelter trees, the desert has won another battle. Their fields lie covered by golden drifts. Then there's the back-breaking work of

The ruined fortress city of Jiaohe. There are many such ruins of lost kingdoms buried in the encroaching sands of the Taklamakan Desert.

clearing it all away and starting over again while the unspoken question nags at them: Will they one day lose their struggle too? Will their little oasis and village, like those cities of long ago, have to give up their life at last to the greedy desert?

Here in western Xinjiang—closer to Mecca, the heart of Islam, than the Hui people—the Uygurs are stricter about their religion. Five times a day they turn to Mecca to offer their prayers. When summer arrives and the harvesting of the wheat is over, the little village has a slack period. Then the Timurs make their annual pilgrimage to Kashi, known in the old days as Kashgar. The women will sell two of the rugs they've woven to a merchant in the city bazaar. At the same time, they'll be able to celebrate the feast of Id Al-Fitr, which marks the end of the sacred period of Ramadan.

There's a bustle in the household as preparations are made. A

This Uygur in an oasis village is building a minaret from which the call for prayer will issue daily. Religion, which was banned in China during the Cultural Revolution, is now allowed.

friend who's not going this year agrees to look after their animals while the Timurs are away. In return the Timurs will take his wife's rugs along with their own, and sell them in Kashi. The couple comes to help load the rugs. Finally father Timur harnesses the two donkeys to the cart. Kunvad and Pelud lift the children onto it. Then the adults climb up. Father Timur, sitting in front, flicks his whip over the donkeys' backs, and off they go at a leisurely pace.

A modern highway now replaces the Old Silk Road. Trucks rumble along it, but most of the travel is still astride a donkey or by cart and donkey. The Timurs are in no hurry. It will take them several days to cover the seventy or so miles to Kashi. But they will break their journey with stops at oases along the way, to visit relatives and friends. They will always be assured a warm welcome, because the Uygurs are a hospitable folk and enjoy entertaining guests.

At last Kashi comes into view, standing proudly on a high mound overlooking the Kizil River. It is a city of only 100,000 people, but it is the largest the Timurs have seen. It is dominated by the great mosque of Id Kah, the center of Islam in China. In Kashi there are women who cover their faces with heavy veils and men who wear long robes.

The narrow roofed-over alleys and poplar-lined streets of the residential district are very quiet, but the newer commercial center is a lively place. Most of the people who are strolling about here are Uygurs. However, there are some other nationalities also—Kazaks, Tadzhiks and Kirghiz—who all follow the Islamic faith. The few non-Moslems among them are people with fair hair and blue eyes. They are descendants of refugee Russians who fled across the border to Xinjiang back in 1917, when the Communists came to power in the Soviet Union.

The small shops that line the streets seem like treasure houses to the Timurs. They stare wide-eyed at the silk dresses, scarves, veils, bolts of cloth, suits, radios, bicycles. . . . Finally they part with some of their little hoard of hard-earned money to buy new dresses for the women, shirts and pants for the men, and outfits for the children.

Down the street they stop before a booth behind which a heavily veiled woman stands selling handmade embroidered Uygur caps. The Timurs purchase cornered ones for the men, round ones for the women.

On the day of Id Al-Fitr, trumpeters standing on the parapet atop the great Id Kah mosque blow their long slender horns, sona horns as they are called, and drummers beat out a lively tattoo. It is a summons to the devout, who gather quickly, dressed in their festival finery. The men stream into the main hall, the women into an anteroom, for the sexes are kept rigidly divided in Moslem mosques.

The congregation kneels on the floor. With heads bowed, the worshipers listen to the chanting of the imam as he performs the ritual that lifts the long fast of Ramadan. When it is over, people flock out of the mosque into the open square before it.

In a twinkling, the sober congregation turns into a merry kaleido-scope of whirling, laughing, singing people. Presently the dancers disperse. The rest of the day is spent exchanging festival greetings with friends and relatives.

The Timurs hurry back to the home of their relatives. Here a banquet has already been spread out on a long runner of cloth laid over the large rug in the living room. The men have prepared a whole roast sheep in the traditional Uygur way. Among the side dishes are noodles, pilaf, vegetables, honey cakes, melons, pears, and figs.

After the meal, father Timur, who has brought along his dutar, begins to play a Uygur courting tune. Soon young couples are jump-ing to their feet to perform the sinuous movements of the provoca-tive dance. Pelud and Kunvad join them. In this magical moment, twisting, turning, flirting as in their courting days, they forget the hard ceaseless work in their fields, the cruel waiting desert. Tonight there is only the joy of the dance, of the festival, of their youth.

Sugula and Drol

Sugula and Drol have grown up together on the grasslands of the Inner Mongolian Autonomous Region, where for generations, their families have lived as nomads with their herds. Mongolia is good pastoral country, troubled only by a scarcity of water. It has an average of thirteen inches of rain a year, and its streams are few and tend to peter out in dry weather. The Mongolians who roam these almost treeless steppes have to carry their water with them in barrels drawn by oxen. And agricultural lands are limited to a few locations, chiefly around the great bend of the Yellow River.

For years these steppes were the home of roving nomads. They were a fierce people who marched to war under the banners of their various tribes. Today nomads still roam the steppes, but the tribes have disappeared. However, the Chinese Mongolians still call their districts Banners.

Mongolia is split into two parts—Outer Mongolia and Inner Mongolia. Outer Mongolia is supposed to be an independent repub-

Above, *in Huhhot, capital of Inner Mongolia, farmers squat behind their trays of fruit and vegetables. All over China, peasants are beginning to bring their vegetables and fruit to sell on the open market. Below, donkeys, horses, oxen, and camels play a big part in transportation within Inner Mongolia.*

lic but is actually a satellite of the Soviet Union. Inner Mongolia, which belongs to China, is divided into Banners. The Banners are subdivided into communes, and the communes, into production units. Each production unit contains several work teams. Some of the teams look after sheep, others herd cattle or horses.

Every year in the summer, after the nomads have sold their fleece and some of their sheep, they pay collective taxes to the government and then divide the rest of the proceeds among themselves. The amount each receives is based on a system of points that are given for work done. Every individual also receives an allotment of grain and meat.

But there are added incentives. Herders who can claim less than a 3 percent death rate among the livestock in their care and at least a 90 percent survival rate among their newborn animals are allowed to keep all those above the quota for their own. In one year, Sugula's family was able to save nineteen additional lambs, which they added to their small private flock. It now numbers forty-eight sheep. They also have several horses, two cows, a calf, and several oxen. Gradually their wealth is increasing.

Sugula's and Drol's families belong to the same work team. Each family is in charge of a thousand sheep. When the pasturage in one area is exhausted, Sugula's and Drol's families move on to new grazing grounds. Because they have to roam about so much, they live in tents which are called yurts. The tents are shaped like great mushrooms. They are made of two layers of felt stretched over a wooden framework. Whenever the pasturage in one area is exhausted, Sugula and Drol help their families pack their belongings in carts. They take down the yurt felts and fold them. Then they take apart the framework of the yurts and strap the individual pieces of wood to the sides of the carts. Finally they harness up the oxen. With the herders on horseback driving the flocks, and the older people and the children taking turns guiding the plodding oxen or getting a ride on the carts, they set off for greener pastures.

From the time they were very young, Sugula and Drol have played and worked together. As soon as they were old enough, they started herding sheep and helping with the lambing. Drol's mother taught her how to shear. Sugula learned how to pass the shorn sheep through the antiseptic spray of the dipping pens.

Drol is an only child. There were six in Sugula's family. But one of his sisters married last year at the age of eighteen and moved away with her husband, and a brother was killed when he was thrown by a horse. Sugula's three youngest siblings stay with their grandparents at the family's winter place. The grandparents have been herders all their lives, but now they have grown too old for a wandering life and have retired. They are supported by Sugula's parents. In turn, the elderly couple cares for the three grandchildren, who attend the nearby primary boarding school but go to their grandparents' home for weekends.

The grandparents live in a three-room brick and stone house in the headquarters town of the production unit. The house, like all the others in the town, was built for them by the production unit with the help of a subsidy from the government, which is encouraging nomads to settle down whenever possible.

Most of the other people who live in the little town belong to a work team that builds sheds, pens, and kunluns. A kunlun is an enclosure protected by low walls to keep the cattle out. The grass in the kunluns is cut periodically and stored away in the sheds. It will be used to tide the livestock over the leanest winter months.

Then there are snows and blinding blizzards, and the bucket-shaped stoves in the yurts glow red with burning chips of dried cattle dung. The chips, which give off an odorless flame, serve for fuel here, as wood is so scarce. Meals are hearty, consisting of steamed millet and noodles and hard cheese and great hunks of half-bloody barbecued mutton. All is washed down with strong tea and fiery drafts of liquor, distilled from fermented ewe's milk. This food fuels the herders, who must wander far and wide searching for scant pasturage for their gaunt flocks, and who must mount long night watches against the ravenous wolves whose howling floats over the steppe-lands.

Finally, when snows grow too deep for the animals to root down to grass, the herders take a brief respite at the headquarters town. Here they drive their animals into pens and feed them the fodder stored in the sheds.

But in these lands not all is harsh. Winter gives way to the green loveliness of spring, spangled with flowers, melodic with the song of the lark. It is a time of plenty. The rich lushness of the following summer draws the nomads north again until the chill of early autumn drives them south once more.

The summer that Sugula turns twenty-one, he and Drol decide they want to spend their lives together. Both families are delighted, for they've been good friends a long while. Preparations for the wedding begin.

In Mongolia, the bride's family provides the dowry. This practice started in the thirteenth century, when a form of Buddhism known as Lamaism spread to Mongolia from Tibet. Lamaism required that at least one son in every family, perhaps more, should enter the monastery, or lamasery as it is known in Tibet and Mongolia, and become a priest, or lama. Lamas were not allowed to marry, and since there were so many of them, there was a surplus of unmarried women. Parents began offering large trousseaux as bribes to get their daughters married.

After the founding of the People's Republic of China, the many privileges, such as full support, which had attracted young men to the lamaseries, were taken away. Many of the lamas left, found work, and married. Today not many young men want to become lamas, and there is no longer a surplus of marriageable young women.

But the brides' parents still follow the practice of giving handsome gifts to the groom. Drol's father and mother purchase a new yurt for the couple, along with quilts and felt floor coverings and a rug. They also present the couple with two wooden trunks which hold a trousseau for the bride and new clothes for the groom.

The day before the wedding, guests begin to arrive. As they enter the reception yurt, which has been set up for the occasion beside the bride's family yurt, they are presented with glasses of strong wine. Toasts are made to the bride and groom. Drol's uncle brings out his horse-headed fiddle with its four strings and begins to sing a betrothal song, his deep-chested baritone rolling out over the steppelands.

As the day progresses, more and more guests arrive. The drinking, the toasting, the singing go on. By sunset the tent is crowded. And the bride's family lays out a feast to feed the hungry guests. Drol's uncle, elder of the family, solemnly picks up a traditional Mongolian knife and cuts a slice from a boiled sheep's head. He puts it in his mouth and eats it, smacking his lips with relish. It is the signal for other guests to start eating too.

The long northern sunset deepens into twilight and then to dusk. The guests have finished the sheep and most of the rest of the food. Another boiled sheep and more food make their appearance, and the drinking and singing continue. Toast after toast is tossed down. The singing, the eating, the boisterous laughter go on till dawn. But neither the bridegroom nor the bride is there to enjoy it.

In her family yurt, where she has spent the night, Drol is dressing for her wedding with the help of her mother and girlfriends. Her bridal robe is of soft, shimmering blue silk, embroidered at the neck and sleeves. Last of all she puts on a filmy scarlet veil that covers her face.

Suddenly there's the distant clatter of hoofs and the neighing of horses. Sugula, who has spent the night in his own family's yurt, is arriving, accompanied by his friends. They reach the bride's yurt and circle it once. Then at the entrance Sugula dismounts. Drol hears him challenging her two bridesmaids, who are standing outside stretching a strip of white felt across the doorway. The girls demand gifts for the bride as the price of entry.

Sugula presents a silver bracelet and a pair of coral earrings, and the girls lower the felt. Sugula strides into the yurt. Through her red veil, Drol sees him standing before her, handsome in his blue silk wedding tunic cinched with a golden belt. His feet are clad in brand-new boots. A scarlet turban is wound round his head. He puts out his hand to her. It is time to go.

Shyly Drol bids her family good-bye and follows Sugula out of the yurt. They mount their horses. Off they gallop to their new home, which has been set up beside Sugula's family yurt. The wedding guests follow, but they can't overtake Sugula and Drol. The two are running a race to see who gets to the yurt first. Mongolian tradition says that the winner of this race will rule the household.

But Sugula and Drol manage to arrive at the same time. They rein in their horses and dismount. Two small bonfires are burning on either side of the entrance to the yurt. Sugula extends his horsewhip to Drol. She takes the other end, and Sugula leads her between the fires into the yurt. Passing through the fires is a symbol of their purity of heart. It also has a more objective purpose—to drive away evil spirits.

The bridegroom's parents are waiting inside to welcome Drol into their family. Sugula's mother lifts the veil from her new daughter-in-law's face. Drol bows to Sugula's parents. Now Sugula is handed a silver wine pot, and Drol is given a tray of cups. Together they begin serving wine, first to Sugula's parents, then to the guests who have followed.

Outside, another great banquet has been spread on a white runner laid over a carpet on the meadow. The feasting and drinking begin again. The merrymaking will continue for several days, without a single thought of sleep by anyone. The hardy Mongolians play as energetically as they ride the steppes.

Shortly afterward, Drol and Sugula and their families prepare for another big event—the great Nadam Fair, which takes place once a year at the end of July. In the Mongolian language, nadam means "recreation." And the fair, which will last from three to five days, is a celebration of the plenty of the year, a joyful interlude before the hard winter arrives. It is a time to barter livestock. Handicrafts and manufactured goods will be on sale. No one would think of going to the fair without bringing along a pouch of money.

Not everyone can attend. A skeleton crew must stay behind to watch over the sheep and cattle. So every year, people have to take turns. This year, Sugula and Drol are going with their families. They set out with their yurts and their carts, driving along the sheep they plan to barter at the fair.

From all directions, other Mongolians are gathering, bringing horses and cattle as well as sheep. A great village of mushroom shapes soon appears on the green meadows. Tall, muscular men, their shoulders broad under tight silk tunics cinched in at the waist with belts or bright sashes, gather in boisterous knots. Women dressed in tunics every color of the rainbow stride with their rolling steppe gait among the yurts. Children scamper underfoot.

Sugula and Drol stroll through the milling crowds with their families, exchanging greetings with friends and relatives they have not seen for a long while. Eventually they join the spectators who line the course where horse races are being held. With a thunder of hoofs, the fleet Mongolian horses are off, bearing riders in brilliant costumes, each determined to win the race and gain the glory, along with one of the prizes—a radio, a woolen blanket, a thermos bottle.

Adult races are followed by races for children. One of Sugula's younger brothers, dressed in the bright new tunic his grandmother has made for him, takes part but loses. He blinks away the tears that would have only brought jeers from his companions and congratulates the winner. His grandmother comforts him with a sweet.

Crowds have gathered around the wrestling matches. Wrestling is a favorite sport in Mongolia. The wrestlers are great brawny men with heavy black boots and colorful, baggy silk pantaloons. Their sleeveless jackets are made of leather or canvas, and around their necks they wear kerchiefs of different colors. The number of colors shows the experience of the wrestler. Red scarves are most common. Few wear the five-colored scarves of the champion.

The wrestlers leap toward each other, flapping their arms like wings, lifting their legs in exaggerated bowlegged steps that resemble the movements of the great grassland eagles. No holds are barred as they kick, butt, grapple, and toss each other around. The contest is over when one or the other is hurled to the ground. And the winner, prancing around the ring to demonstrate his victory, prepares to take on the next challenger.

When the sun's beams lie level over the steppes, the crowds break for the evening meal. Sugula and Drol can join the other members of their work team at a communal supper, but they prefer going to one of the small family-run restaurants that have been set up on the grounds.

Afterward the men and women drift apart. Sugula and his father go to the animal pens to barter some of their sheep for a couple of horses. The other members of the family stroll from booth to booth, marveling over the sewing machines, wristwatches, bicycles, bolts of cloth, and radios, which clerks have brought from the big Beijing department stores to sell here.

Drol and her mother and mother-in-law are attracted by the colorful silks and brocades. Drol's father stops before a display of long-bladed knives with worked metal handles, made by Mongolian craftsmen. All are sharp enough to slice through a whole cooked sheep. He tests several, and finally selects the one he wants. Then he goes off to join one of the convivial groups that are gathering for boisterous merrymaking, which will last well into the night.

The womenfolk are drawn from the booths by the clear sweet voices of a professional song-and-dance troupe which has begun to put on an outdoor performance. They watch for a while, then move away to an open-air movie with the dialogue dubbed in the Mongolian language. They sit on the grass to watch it with the rest of the crowd. The women seldom get to see a film, and this one fascinates them.

On the last day, the cavalry of the People's Liberation Army together with the militia put on a joint equestrian show, which is the highlight of the fair. The crowds along the course break into raucous cheers as the handsome horses and their bareback riders thunder down the plain in battle formation. As they go, the men raise gleaming swords that flash now right, now left, slashing through standing twigs with unerring aim, knocking stuffed bags off posts, flipping rattan wreaths off stakes and tossing them into the air.

A display of marksmanship follows. Riding at breakneck speed, the men raise their rifles to shoot down multicolored balloons released into the sky. Roar after roar of approval rises from the crowds.

Dusk of this last night is heralded by the bursting of firecrackers accompanied by the laughing shrieks of the children who have set them off. When darkness obliterates the land, the fireworks begin. Reds, greens, golds, glistening whites, clusters and great spangles bloom far overhead.

Sugula and Drol, their hands tightly clasped, watch awestruck as the fountains of multicolored lights burst against the black sky, drowning out the stars. This brilliant spectacle marks a fitting end to the Nadam Fair. But for Sugula and Drol, it also heralds the beginning of a long life together.

The Roof
of the World

Astride their rangy horses, Retso and her husband Ngawang drive
a small herd of yaks through the high pasturelands of the Tibetan
Autonomous Region. The great shaggy creatures, relatives of the
North American bison, amble along in single file. They have just
been cut out of a larger herd that the couple has left temporarily in
the care of Ngawang's mother.

Domesticated yaks, most of them crossbred with lowland cows to
improve their flesh and milk, are one of the few animals that can
thrive in these high altitudes, for this is the Roof of the World. The
great plateau ranges from 5,000 to 20,000 feet above sea level and
is enclosed by towering mountains, among them the Himalayas,
which bar the way to India.

Flocks of sheep are kept in the lower Tibetan valleys. But the yaks
can survive in the higher elevations. Even on soaring mountain
passes, the sure-footed, great-chested yaks are capable of carrying

Two Tibetan girls gather brush for cooking fuel. They are wearing warm Han Chinese jackets and sneakers.

heavy loads. At altitudes where horses would drop dead of heart failure, yaks can be pressed into service as mounts. They also provide clothing and most of the Tibetans' food, in the form of milk, yogurt, butter, and meat.

Retso and her husband are going down to Lhasa, capital of Tibet, which lies in a valley that is still some 12,000 feet above sea level. Two of their yaks will end in the cattle yards on the outskirts of the city. There Retso and Ngawang will barter some of the meat with the butchers who will slaughter their animals and then render them into cuts.

Two other yaks are serving as beasts of burden. One is laden with containers holding rich yak butter churned by Retso and her mother-in-law. It is a yak cow, which can also provide the couple with milk during their stay in Lhasa. The other yak carries food supplies, and poles and a canvas sheet for a lean-to tent.

Retso and Ngawang will pitch their tent at the entrance to the old marketplace, along with other herders and peasants who have come to sell their goods on the open market. Here vendors of all kinds line the narrow unpaved streets, which are hemmed in by three-story medieval stone houses.

Ngawang will take his place among them, displaying his freshly butchered bloody cuts for the Lhasa folk. Retso will squat beside her containers of yak butter. At a customer's request, she will carefully ladle out chunks of the waxy-looking stuff and weigh it on her small scales. If a lump should fall to the ground, Retso will just pick it up and brush it off.

With the money they receive, Retso and Ngawang will purchase a new supply of barley flour from the peasants. Roasted barley flour is the staple of the Tibetans' diet. Retso and Ngawang have brought some, as well as a compact tea brick, a small portable brazier, a bag of dried yak chips for fuel, butter, and two bowls. Along with milk from their yak, this is all that is necessary to prepare their national dish, called tsamba. They make a thick brew of the strong tea, mix it with milk, slap in a chunk of yak butter, pour in some barley flour, and use fingers to stir the concoction into a thick paste. They roll the dough into balls, one at a time, and pop them into their mouths.

Retso and Ngawang plan to spend several days in Lhasa. They aren't coming just on business; they also want to take part in the National Day celebrations. National Day is one of the biggest holidays of the year. It falls on the first of October. On this date back in 1949, Mao Zedong announced the founding of the People's Republic of China.

For months the couple has been looking forward to this brief respite in their hard life. Retso is clothed in her holiday attire, which is in large part her everyday dress as well. The dark brown voluminous robe, woven of yak hair, which she is wearing is called a shuba. It is cinched in at the waist with a stout cloth tie. The right shoulder and sleeve are cut away, exposing a red blouse underneath.

Retso's hair, shiny with yak butter, is dressed in dozens of slender braids tied with red ribbons. Silver and turquoise bracelets and earrings jangle as she rides. They are heirlooms passed down through generations, as is the silver amulet box that hangs around her neck. The box contains slips of paper with prayers to Buddha printed on them. Buddhism is an ancient faith in Tibet, and Retso is an ardent Buddhist.

Ngawang wears a short cape. Unkempt black locks frame his sunburnt face, which is shadowed under a wide-brimmed hat. Long necklaces of coral and turquoise intertwined are looped around his neck. His feet are clad in felt riding boots with upturned toes.

Retso and Ngawang and their worn clothes are all impregnated with dust and rancid yak butter and human sweat. Water is scarce here. It comes from melting snows and glaciers in the high mountains, and flows icy cold through the valleys. The herders seldom wash their clothing or themselves. To bathe is to run the risk of catching pneumonia. Though the Tibetans have adapted to high altitudes from birth, they are still susceptible to bitter cold or dust storms. Then their lungs can become congested and filled with liquid, bringing on a serious form of pneumonia.

A young Tibetan herder from the back country in typical shuba and felt boots.

Winds are fierce on these uplands. They sweep across the high country with a mighty force that tosses large boulders about like tumbleweed and turns day into yellow twilight. Retso remembers the last big gale. Sturdy yaks huddled together, their shaggy backs to the wind, while she and Ngawang and his mother sheltered in their tent, which was straining against the wind like the billowing sails of a ship, in danger at any minute of being blown away. Through the long howling hours, Retso and the old woman kept vigorously twirling their prayer wheels. Like Retso's amulet box, the wheels contain strips of printed prayers. The women firmly believed that with every turn of the wheel, those prayers went flying off to Buddha, seeking protection against the demons in the wind. Outside they could hear the strips of prayer cloth, which they kept tied to the roof and poles of their tent, flapping out incantations also. And they were reassured.

Today the air is stirred by only a light breeze. Bright sunlight streams down from a rich blue sky. Great billows of white cloud arch their backs along the southern horizon. This day is a gift from Buddha, Retso thinks joyfully. As the couple nears Lhasa, the familiar landmark of the Potala looms against the skyline. It stands as though rooted there on a craggy cliff some 700 feet high. The thirteen tiers of its cream- and maroon-colored walls are topped by gilded tile roofs and golden steeples that gleam against the burnished sky.

The Potala was the home of generations of Buddhist priest-kings who ruled Tibet under the title of Dalai Lama. Buddhist priests were forbidden to marry, so the Dalai Lamas had no children to whom they could pass along their kingdom. Instead they were said to possess a single soul—the soul of a Living Buddha, or Enlightened One.

Each time a Dalai Lama died, it was believed the soul of the Living Buddha would pass into the body of a newborn baby. Following the death of an old Dalai Lama, his advisers would go out in search of the reborn Living Buddha. The lamas would visit families

Above, *the Potala rises in splendor above a moat.* Below, *Lhasa, the capital of Tibet, viewed from the roof of the Potala.*

where a son had been born in a cowshed, since that was one of the signs of the Living Buddha. When they found such a baby, they would check to see if he also fulfilled other secret criteria. If so, they would present him with a few objects, among which were some that had once belonged to the old Dalai Lama. If the child did not reach for any of these articles, the lamas would continue their search. If he did reach, they were sure they had found the Living Buddha. They would bring him back to the Potala, where he lived a lonely life in the thousand rooms of his palace. Here he was watched over and trained by attendant lamas who ruled the country for him until he reached the age of sixteen and began governing in his own name. As a Living Buddha, the Dalai Lama was held in awe by all Tibetans, and his word was accepted as law.

Throughout the centuries, Tibet has sometimes been independent; at other times it has been either a protectorate of China or ruled by it. In 1950, after the founding of the People's Republic, the People's Liberation Army entered Tibet. In 1951, Beijing and the Dalai Lama signed an agreement that granted the Dalai Lama the right to rule Tibet his way, while Beijing handled the country's foreign affairs and promised to protect it against invasion. Keeping Tibet free of foreign powers, particularly the Soviet Union, is very important to China, because whoever gets control of the Roof of the World would be in a position to threaten China's low-lying lands to the east.

The Tibetans, however, wanted complete independence. They staged a revolt in 1956. It was unsuccessful, and the Dalai Lama, fearing for his life, fled to India with many of his followers. Though the Chinese government has extended an invitation to him, he has not returned since. Today the great empty Potala is a museum, and the old-style Tibetan government has been abolished in favor of socialism.

Retso and Ngawang are among many Tibetans who want the Dalai Lama to come back. But they would not care to live the kind of life they have heard about from some of the old herders who were

A street scene in old Lhasa. The man wearing the devil mask has set his neighbor to saying his Buddhist beads. The sagging front of the devil man's shuba is filled with everything from cooking utensils to food.

slaves in the early days. Then most of the land was owned by lamas, noblemen, or government officials, and most of the people worked for them as serfs or slaves. All was well if their masters were kind, but many were brutal. Retso and Ngawang have seen elderly people with one eye gouged out or the stump of an arm where the right hand was amputated as punishment for displeasing a master.

There are 300,000 men of the People's Liberation Army stationed in Tibet, with about 100,000 in Lhasa itself. Lhasa also has a large number of civilian Hans. Some are doctors, others technicians and factory workers. At first, most government officials were Hans. But many were not happy in Tibet, partly because they were affected by the high altitude. And when their initial period of duty, which was to be limited to five years, was extended to fifteen or even twenty, they became bitter. In turn, the Tibetans resented the Hans, who, they felt, did not understand their culture and traditions and in some cases despised them.

During the Cultural Revolution, hard feelings between the Hans and Tibetans reached a breaking point. Blind directives issued from Beijing ordered the Tibetans to slaughter most of their livestock and convert pastoral lands to wheat fields, under the slogan Make Grain the Priority. In most places the altitude was too high for this. The crops failed, and the deep plowing destroyed the natural ground cover. Good pastureland was turned into dreary wastes eroded by wind and rain. With the loss of their yaks, on which they depended so much for food, the people came close to mass starvation.

After the overthrow of the Gang of Four, the government moved to make up for the wrongs done the Tibetans. It gave them full control of their farms and pastoral lands, and encouraged them to replenish their livestock. It lifted state taxes until they could get on their feet again, and it released them from having to meet quotas or sell their produce to the government unless they chose to do so. And it is pouring more money into Tibet than into any other part of the country, in an effort to improve the poor economic conditions. But it is doubtful whether this high tableland with its fragile ecology will ever be self-sufficient.

The government is also trying to heal another deep rift between Tibetans and Hans. After the crushing of the 1956 revolt, many lamas were forced out of the lamaseries, a number of which were closed. The Tibetans, most of whom were deeply religious, were discouraged from worshiping. Things became much worse during the Cultural Revolution. Then Red Guards rampaged across Tibet, defacing or destroying many of the region's remaining temples and historic lamaseries. Almost all the rest of the lamas were evicted, and worship of any kind was not only discouraged but strictly forbidden.

Now the government has lifted the ban against religion. It has allocated 2 million yuan to restore some of the monasteries that were badly defaced and is permitting former lamas to return. Once more, temples are open to the public, and maroon-robed, shaven-headed priests chant their litanies inside the sacred walls.

One of Tibet's holiest temples, the Jokan, which stands in the heart of Lhasa, was spared. Pilgrims from all over Tibet and even from other provinces are again coming to worship here. Most of them are peasants, pastoralists, or older persons. Few educated young people believe in Buddha.

Retso and Ngawang, who find ghosts and demons in the wild forces of nature, visit the temple. They join the long line of chanting pilgrims who carry yak-butter candles to place on the altar, and afterward prostrate themselves before the golden Buddha, gift of the Tang princess, Wen Cheng. In A.D. 641, Wen Cheng came as a bride to King Songzanganbu, bringing Buddhism with her to Tibet.

While Retso and Ngawang are in the temple, people all over Lhasa are preparing for the coming holiday. At two o'clock in the afternoon, factories and schools close. Young factory women, both Han and Tibetan, hurry home to put finishing touches on the new dresses or blouses they will be wearing tomorrow. Women bustle about their kitchens, preparing picnic dishes for the morning.

The picnic grounds are in Norbu Linka Park, which lies just outside Lhasa. The wide vistas of landscaped lawns, shade trees, and brilliant flower beds were once part of the Dalai Lama's summer estate. The park is now open to the public, while the palace in which he stayed has been turned into a museum.

With the dawn of National Day, people begin streaming to the park. All kinds of people—peasants, pastoralists, city folk, Tibetans, Hans—arrive on foot, by bus, by bicycle, in yak-drawn carts, in trucks. They stagger through the gates, burdened down with huge picnic hampers containing little cakes and cookies, bottled soft drinks, and quantities of strong wine distilled from fermented barley mash. Some bring great iron pots containing a stew of vegetables and mutton chunks. Others carry blankets, clotheslines, and pillows.

The clotheslines are quickly strung up around trees, marking out rectangles. Blankets are hung on the lines at breast level. Inside the rectangle, other blankets are spread on the grass, and pillows are strewn about. Picnic stuffs are spread out. And families sit or recline, munching on food, exchanging news and gossip. Now and then acquaintances passing by look over the blanket screens and stick out their tongues in the Tibetan form of greeting.

In a short while, the green vistas of parkland have given way to a surging sea of people that eddies around the roped-off rectangles. Some of the city folk are wearing the typical jacket and trousers of the Han Chinese. Most of the children are dressed in holiday finery. Young factory girls, strolling about in clusters, are wearing the long dresses they have just finished sewing. Their elegant gowns and smooth, rosy-cheeked complexions contrast sharply with the dull gray or brown shubas and the rough, chapped faces of herders and lumbermen.

Even Gezhu and his eighteen-year-old son Chile are here. They've come by truck all the way from their lumber camp in the virgin forests that clothe the lower slopes of the Himalayas. The forests are the home of leopards, deer, the mild black bear, and the great brown bear as fierce as any grizzly. Chile's ravaged face, from which the nose has been bitten, tells of his encounter with one of the savage beasts.

This is a day of triumph for twenty-nine-year-old Ngapoi Tudandanda, descendant of one of Tibet's noble families. Once he would have been a lord. Now he has just achieved his dearest dream—to become a member of the Chinese Communist Party, from which he was barred during the Cultural Revolution. He not only has been made a member in good standing, but also holds a clerk's job with the government. He looks on it as the first step in his climb upward.

Ngapoi swaggers a bit as, with cheeks flushed from barley wine and pride, he offers his mother a plate of tidbits. The huge old woman reclines languidly on a heap of pillows, her billowing form encased in a tentlike gown. She accepts the plate, smiling indulgently up at her son. Let him bask in this moment of triumph, she thinks. What does he know of real power? In her youth she tasted it, a heady experience. She's content now to let the world go by.

In another enclosure, twenty-year-old Dochen has her own dream. She's a peasant from a nearby commune, pretty in her best holiday dress—the traditional Tibetan blouse, dark woolen vest, and long woolen skirt with its apron of multicolored horizontal stripes. Her plaited hair is coiled round her head. Her face is chapped by wind and sun and flushed from altitude. Her hands are rough from bringing in the autumn wheat crop.

Dochen's eyes shine with her dream. One day soon, her commune has promised, mechanization will come to the fields in the form of a bright red harvester that will do some of the work of reaping. And Dochen has been told she will be taught how to drive that harvester and how to service it and, if necessary, make repairs on it. To Dochen, this will mark the height of achievement.

Tsama, safe among her family now, feels pride mixed with apprehension as she looks into the future. Tsama is in her last year of senior middle school this year, and her teachers have told her she's been selected to go to the Institute for National Minorities at Chengde when she graduates. There are ten National Minority Institutes in the country. They train selected minority young people in different skills which they can take back to their homes.

Tsama wants to be an agriculturalist, experimenting with different strains of wheat to evolve those that are most adaptable to high altitudes. She also wants to work on the development of tough perennial forage grass, so that the eroded pasturelands can be re-

This old woman has journeyed from afar to enjoy the National Day picnic.

seeded. Tsama knows she must go to the institute to learn how to do these things. But she has never left home before, and the thought of traveling so far and living among strangers frightens her. She has heard, too, that Tibetans suffer as much from lowland sickness as the lowland people suffer from altitude sickness, and she wonders if this will affect her studies.

The afternoon shadows lengthen over the trampled grass. People begin taking down their blankets and clotheslines, gathering up their picnic pots and baskets and their children. A steady stream heads for the exit gates. But there are many others who will stay late into the night. Free-flowing liquor has loosened their tongues and feet. Someone begins playing a lively tune on his fiddle. Others start singing. A folk dance begins and grows wilder and wilder.

Retso and Ngawang join the others in the lusty dance. Retso's braids swirl round her head. Under his wide-brimmed hat, Ngawang's unkempt hair flaps like black wings. Round and round, Retso's skirts go whirling, Ngawang's boots go clicking, kicking. Arms akimbo, they'll dance and drink and sing until they've wrung the last joys out of this brief holiday. Then on the following morning, putting fun behind them, they'll be on their way back to the bleak pastoral lands.

Great Proletarian Cultural
Revolution, *cont'd.*
students' role in, 15, 16,
21–22
in Tibet, 124, 125
violence created by, 15, 16
youth scarred by, 13, 21–
22
Greek traders, 99–100
Gu Ernang, 67–78
army registration of, 73–74
home of, 68–69
as militia volunteer, 71
schooling of, 70–71
as soldier, 74–78

handicrafts, 6, 62
Hangzhou, 39
Han nationality:
dynasty of, 80
Hui animosity toward, 88–90
as majority people, *vi,* 92
silk trade and, 99–100
Tibetans' animosity toward,
124–125
Harbin, 46
health care:
acupuncture used in, 64
doctor shortage and, 45, *54*
herbal medicines used in, 64
illness and, mental and
emotional, 28
midwifery in, 64–65
neighborhood committee
services in, 27–28
in villages, 61, 63–64
workers' benefits and, 8–9
Himalaya Mountains, 115, 126
hospitals, poor conditions in, 28,
63, *63*
housing:
factory-provided, 1, 10
of nomads, 107, 108–109
running water in, 13, 62–63
shortages in cities, 26, 34, *35*

housing, *cont'd.*
shortages in villages, 71
Hua Guofeng, 18
Huangpu River, 1–2
Hui nationality, 87–91
Han animosity toward, 88–90
physical characteristics of,
87–88, *89*
religion of, 87–90
Hu Jiangsu, 79–91
beloved of, 87–91
Changan visited by, 80–82
as university student, 83–91
hydroelectric power, 57, 75

Id Al-Fitr, feast of, 101–104
Id Kah, mosque of, 103
India, 76, 115, 122
Inner Mongolia, 105–107, *116*
Inner Mongolian Autonomous
Region, 105
irrigation, 59, 95

Japan, China invaded by, 53, 73,
90
Jiang Qing, 15, 16, 17, 18, 21
Jokan (Tibetan temple), 125

Kashi, 102–104
Kazak nationality, 103
Kirghiz nationality, 103
Kizil River, 103
Kunlun range, 95
Kuomintang, 72–73

Lamaism, 109, 124–125
Lanzhou, *70,* 74–76
Lao, Old Auntie, 13, 16, 18–22,
24–26, 34
childhood of, 21–22
disputes mediated by, 26
Lhasa, 117–129, *121, 123*
holiday celebration in, 118,
125–129
marketplace in, 117–118

Northern Campaign, 72

Old Silk Road, 102
Outer Mongolia, 105–107
overpopulation, 37, *39*, 66, 97

Pamir Range, 95
Parsee traders, 99–100
People's Liberation Army, 15,
    16, 17, 71–78, 113–114
  earthquake relief work of, 42
  farming activities of, 74
  history of, 72–73, 74
  Hui goodwill toward, 88–89
  peasants' goodwill toward, 73,
    74
  in Tibet, 122, 124
  women in, 75
People's Republic of China:
  founding of, 2, 51, 53, 73
  government of, 16
  Han-Hui relations improved
    by, 90
  National Day in, 118,
    125–129
  religion in, ban against, *102*,
    109, 125
  Tibetan independence and,
    122–124
Persia, 81, 95, 99–100
pollution, 3
Potala, 120–122, *121*
prayer wheels, 120
private enterprise, Cultural
    Revolution and, 17, 19
pronunciation, guide to, *vii*

Qin Shi Huang Di, dynasty of,
    80, 81, *83*

radio broadcasts, 3, 34–35
Ramadan, sacred period of,
    101–104
Red Army, 72–73, 74, 88–89
Red Guards, 15–16

religions:
  ban against, *102*, 109, 125
  Buddhism, 76–78, *77*, *78*, 93,
    98, 120–125, *123*
  Islam, 87–90, 93, 98, 101–104
  Lamaism, 109, 124–125
Retso (Tibetan), 115–129
  holiday celebrated by, 118,
    125–129
  yak herds of, 115–117
revolutionary committees, 17–18
Roman traders, 99–100
Roof of the World, 115, 122

sanitation, 13, 62–63
schools, schooling, *44*
  Cultural Revolution and,
    16–17, 21–22
  night classes in, 45–46
  opportunity for, 17, *65*
  teacher shortage in, 65
  in villages, 61, 65–66, 70–71
  for workers, 8
  see also universities
Shanghai, 1–22, *4*
  Communists massacred in, 72
  Cultural Revolution in, 16
  entertainment in, 28–30
  foreigners expelled from, 2
  parks in, 11–12, *12*
  restaurants in, *20*, 29–30, *29*
  smog problem in, 3
  unemployment in, 2, 19, *20*
Shanghai Machine Tools
    Factory, 2–10
  employees' housing at, 1, 9–10
  government ownership of, 7
  production contests in, 5–7
  trade unions in, 8, 9
  workers' benefits in, 8–9
  workers' carelessness in, 7
Shanghai Travel Service, 39
Shanmin (Liu Baolang's friend),
    45–46, 53–54
Shen Tiyi, 21–22